A Word Write Now

A Thematic Thesaurus for Stylized Writing

Illustrated by:
Celina Barndt
Zechariah Romo
James Schwacofer

Discovering just the right word to use while improving one's writing skills becomes an intriguing search for those who may need a large selection of easy-to-locate, quality word choices to spur them on. May A Word *Write* Now offer that pearl of inspiration.

Second Edition © June 2010
Loranna Schwacofer

Dedication

A Word *Write* Now is dedicated to all those for whom words take extra time—time to hear accurately, time to carefully reflect upon, and time to thoughtfully choose which to speak and, even more challenging, which to commit to paper.

Words are vital in our everyday life, and learning to love them and respect their power to harm or heal is also vital in determining the quality of our life experiences. It is the hope of this author that those who use this book will be inspired to treasure the value of words and how they can be wisely and freely used to share one's thoughts and feelings, convey truth, and stand firmly for that which is right.

Acknowledgements

Special thanks to Holly Cohen for her insight, suggestions, and valuable input,
to my husband, Randy, for his encouragement and patience
throughout the writing and editing process,
to my family members for their input and assistance along the way,
to Andrew Pudewa and his dedicated team to whom I am deeply grateful,
and most of all, to the students I served who
gave me the inspiration to write for them.

Copyright © 2006 by Loranna Schwacofer
ISBN-10: 0-9779860-0-4
ISBN-13: 978-0-9779860-0-2
Second Edition 2010
Published by Institute for Excellence in Writing

All rights reserved. No part of this book may be reproduced, stored in a retrieval system, or transmitted in any form or by any means, electronic, mechanical, photocopying, recording, or otherwise, without the prior written permission of the author, except as provided by USA copyright law and the specific policy below.

Home use: You may freely copy our materials for use by multiple children within your immediate family, or purchase additional books so all children have one of their own.
Small group or co-op classes: Each participating student or family is required to purchase a book.
Classroom teachers: Each teacher and student should purchase his or her own book.
Library use: Printed materials may be checked out, provided patrons agree not to make copies.

Additional copies of the complete workbook can be ordered from:
Institute for Excellence in Writing
8799 N. 387 Rd.
Locust Grove, OK 74352
tel. 800.856.5815 fax 603.925.5123
info@excellenceinwriting.com
www.excellenceinwriting.com

A Word *Write* Now

Table of Contents

Introduction to A Word *Write* Now 1
An Overview of A Word *Write* Now 2
Simple Definitions of Parts of Speech 4

SECTION A - Character Traits 7
    Introduction to Character Traits 8
    Words for Anger 10
    Words for Cheerfulness 12
    Words for Compassion 14
    Words for Complaining 16
    Words for Courage 18
    Words for Criticism 20
    Words for Curiosity 22
    Words for Dishonesty 24
    Words for Envy 26
    Words for Exuberance 28
    Words for Fearfulness 30
    Words for Generosity 32
    Words for Gossip 34
    Words for Honor 36
    Words for Hostility 38
    Words for Humility 40
    Words for Lawlessness 42
    Words for Laziness 44
    Words for Obedience 46
    Words for Pride 48
    Words for Responsibility 50
    Words for Stubbornness 52
    Words for Wisdom 54
    Open Form for Student Originality 56

SECTION B - Descriptive Words 59
    Words to Describe Appearance 60
    Words to Describe Color 62
    Words to Describe Size 64
    Words to Describe Time 66
    Words to Describe Temperature 70
    Words to Describe Texture 72
    Words to Describe Shape 73

A Word *Write* Now

Table of Contents

SECTION C - Words for Movement and the Senses 75
    Words for Feet 76
    Words for Hands 78
    Words for Hearing 80
    Words for Seeing 82
    Words for Smelling 84
    Words for Speaking 86
    Words for Thinking 88

SECTION D - Appendix 91
    Playing with Words - Make It Fun 92
    Transitions Not Related to Time 94
    Prepositions - Excellent for Memorization 95
    Categories of Literary Genres 96
    Definitions and Examples of Literary Devices 98

BIBLIOGRAPHY 103

A Word *Write* Now

INTRODUCTION

Teachers, home schooling parents, and students long for materials that encourage excellence in writing in an easy to use, interesting, and upbeat way. A Word *Write* Now has been created to encourage writers of any age to delight in playing with words in order to improve the quality of their written expression while developing their own unique styles of writing.

In A Word *Write* Now, the words are organized specifically to make it easier for students to find an appropriate group of words from which to choose. Often students will not have *any* particular word in mind to replace an overused word or to better describe something. First they must be able to decide what category or type of word for which they are looking. For example, do they need a word to describe how something looks, feels, smells, or are they looking for a motion made by someone, or perhaps an attitude? Writing will improve as words that *show*, not *tell* are selected.

Once students have become familiar with the layout and content of A Word *Write* Now, they will be able to work independently and quickly find the right category or list of words they want. Each category includes words grouped and color-coded by nouns, adjectives, adverbs, verbs, and sometimes phrases, as well as a personalized section, Additional Words, for students to add their own words. Searching for just the right word becomes an engaging and exciting activity, with endless creative possibilities, also leading to better usage of a thesaurus and quality writing. To further delight the reader, there are definitions, related quotes by famous people, and excerpts from classical literature included along with each trait.

A Word *Write* Now is organized into four sections:

1. Section A: Character Traits
    Section A features an introduction to the importance of characters in a story and a preview list of traits. This is followed by 23 character traits which include lists of words categorized by nouns, adjectives, adverbs, verbs, phrases and Additional Words. Here students will also find famous quotations related to the trait, under the heading: "Thoughts on . . .," a definition of the trait, and rich, pertinent excerpts from literature, encouraging students to observe the stylish writing techniques of famous authors and to seek out quality literature to read and imitate in their writing.

2. Section B: Words to Describe
    Here are lists of descriptive words for appearance, color, size, time, temperature, texture, and shape.

3. Section C: Words for Movement and the Senses
    Look for word lists for the actions of feet, hands, hearing, seeing, smelling, speaking and thinking in this section.

4. Section D: Appendix
    Included is an extensive list of common literary devices with sentence examples of each, as well as lists of words for transitions, prepositions, and literary genres.

An Overview of A Word Write Now

Section A: Character Traits

Section A begins with an *Introduction to Character Traits,* giving the reader a quick peek at how to develop characters in fiction, as well as a preview list of descriptive adjectives for a variety of traits. This gives one a sense of the extent and range of human emotions and behavior patterns common to man, while developing a rich vocabulary and inspiring depth and precision to writing activities.

There are twenty-three traits listed in **Section A**, with other important ones to be discovered and added by the reader. Becoming familiar with the parts of speech is so important in using A Word *Write* Now, that there are simple definitions found on pages four and five. It is worth noting that when a writer is familiar with the parts of speech, he or she will find that it is easy to change the endings on most of the words to then use them as a different part of speech. For example: *affection* is a noun, *affectionate* an adjective, and *affectionately* an adverb. Therefore, one can experience a great deal of freedom to develop one's own unique style of writing, while keeping it rich and lively. The richness of language used by renowned authors *will* inspire budding writers when they read the *Excerpts from Classical Literature* located throughout this section.

> "Character cannot be developed in ease and quiet. Only through experience of trial and suffering can the soul be strengthened, vision cleared, ambition inspired and success achieved."
>
> (Helen Keller)

Section B: Words to Describe

Words to describe things are usually introduced in the early grades but remain important for writers of all ages. Many children begin to expand their vocabulary by using descriptive words. This is a good place to start students on their stimulating journey of playing with words. There is plenty of content here with which to practice. This section lends itself well to factual paragraph and report writing but also is important in writing fiction. Remember, **Section B** includes *words to describe: appearance, color, size, time, shape, temperature, and texture.* There is no end to descriptive words in our language. Try using a thesaurus to extend these lists, adding categories such as "rate of movement" (how fast or slow objects are moving) to the **Additional Words** section. Learning to categorize words is an excellent skill for all students to develop, making it much easier to find the needed word at a moment's notice.

Section C: Words for Movement and the Senses

Words for Movement and the Senses includes word choices related to particular actions primarily made by people. There is more variety of categories and titles here than in the other sections. Further explorations in a thesaurus might include looking for actions of animals, vehicles, or objects in space. Some words are more limited in their usage than others. Section C includes *words for moving our feet, hands, words for smelling, hearing, seeing, speaking, and thinking.* This section provides lots of opportunities for practicing the skills of labeling and classifying information, which, again, helps students quickly locate the right word.

Section D: Specialized Tools for Writing Well

When writing, especially fiction, it is important to have a good foundational knowledge of common writing terms, common structures to follow, and common stylistic techniques from which to choose. While A Word *Write* Now is primarily designed to offer excellent word choices and to provide those words in structured categories, some basic reference information may lighten the load for those who need refreshing on such topics as:

    **simple definitions of the basic parts of speech*, located on pages four and five
    *transitional words to lead the reader from one concept to the next
    **a list of prepositions and prepositional phrases*

and for students who want further intriguing challenges:

    *a set of 19 *definitions and examples of literary devices* from which to choose to further develop their unique style of writing. These have been presented in an easy-to-understand, lighthearted manner. They provide a great way to end a book on words and simply shouldn't be overlooked!

Discovering Other Valuable Tools in A Word *Write* Now

With careful observation, A Word *Write* Now will provide even richer experiences in appreciating the power and impact words have on the reader. Most pages have related, famous quotations and a variety of excerpts from classical literature, stimulating interest in reading and helping students make important connections between the concepts they read and those they might choose to express in writing. Special effort has been made to avoid repetition of verses or book titles. There are over 70 novel, short story, or poem titles included. Enjoy reading these aloud and discussing why they are under a certain section and category.

Simple Definitions of Parts of Speech

NOUN: Names a person, place, thing or idea.
　　Try using *the* or *some* in front of a word to see if the word is a common noun.
　　　　The <u>bouquet</u> smelled lovely.   *Some <u>people</u> enjoy playing with <u>words</u>.*

COMMON NOUN: Names every day terms for people, places, things or ideas.
　　The <u>people</u> were ice skating in the <u>city</u>.

PROPER NOUN: Gives the name of a specific person, place, thing or idea.

　　<u>Abraham Lincoln</u> loved to use language to play jokes on others.
　　The <u>Lincoln</u> family loved to ice skate with friends in <u>City Park</u>.

PRONOUN: Takes the place of a noun. It can be singular or plural. Put a pronoun
　　　　in the place of a noun and see if the sentence makes sense.
　Singular pronouns used as a subject include: I, you, he, she, it.
　Plural pronouns used as a subject include: we, you, they.
　Other pronouns include: me, you, him, her, it and the plurals: us, you, them.

　　<u>They</u> skated with <u>them</u> every Sunday afternoon.

ADJECTIVE: Describes a noun or a pronoun. Test for an adjective by saying:
　　the _____ person   or   *a _____ object*   or   *an _____ idea*

　It can answer the questions:
　　　What kind of?   Which?   How many?   How much?

　　That was a <u>refreshing</u> thought.

　　The <u>five</u> students will play <u>this</u> Category Game.

VERB: A word that shows action, existence (being), or an occurrence.

　To tell if a word is an action verb, try using "I . . ." in front of it.

　　　I <u>thought</u>.   *I <u>commented</u>.*   *I <u>viewed</u>.*

　A verb can also show a state of being or can link other words together.
　Helping verbs can also be linking verbs. These are also linking or being verbs:
　　<u>am</u>, <u>is</u>, <u>are</u>, <u>was</u>, <u>were</u>, <u>be</u>, <u>being</u>, <u>been</u>, <u>become</u>, <u>seem</u>

　　　I <u>am</u>.   *I <u>was</u>.*   *They <u>were</u>.*   *She <u>was</u> it.*

ADVERB: Describes a verb, an adjective, or another adverb.

It can answer these questions about the verb being described:

How?…………...*Eagerly opening the book, she shouted, "Words!"*

When?…………..*She immediately began to turn the pages.*

Where?…….…...*She sat there for a long time.*

To what extent?...*She inspected it thoroughly.*

It can answer this question about the adjective being described:

How?…………...*The brightly colored pages drew her attention.*

It can answer these questions about the adverb being described:

How?…………...*She read the Hostile Shark word lists rather carefully.*

How much?…….*There she found a quite chillingly accurate word choice for her newly created villain.*

PREPOSITION: A word that shows a relationship of a noun or pronoun to another word in the sentence.

It is almost always the first word or words of a prepositional phrase.

Because prepositions are so unique and important to understand, you will find all of page 95 in A Word*Write* Now devoted to them. Try committing them to memory.

Here's an activity to help find the subject and the verb of any sentence:

First, find all the prepositional phrases in a sentence and cross them out. When they are removed from the sentence, it is much easier to find the subject and the verb of the sentence.

Here is an example: "One prepositional phrase is ~~in this sentence~~."

A Quotation to Inspire Your Writing

"Words are things, and a small drop of ink, falling like dew upon a thought, produces that which makes thousands, perhaps millions think."

(Lord Byron)

Simple Definitions of Parts of Speech   5

Section A
Character Traits

Introduction to Character Traits 8
Words for Anger 10
Words for Cheerfulness 12
Words for Compassion 14
Words for Complaining 16
Words for Courage 18
Words for Criticism 20
Words for Curiosity 22
Words for Dishonesty 24
Words for Envy 26
Words for Exuberance 28
Words for Fearfulness 30
Words for Generosity 32
Words for Gossip 34
Words for Honor 36
Words for Hostility 38
Words for Humility 40
Words for Lawlessness 42
Words for Laziness 44
Words for Obedience 46
Words for Pride 48
Words for Responsibility 50
Words for Stubbornness 52
Words for Wisdom 54
Open Form for Student Originality 56

Introduction to Character Traits

Quotations to Inspire Your Writing

Here are excerpts from Teaching the Classics by Adam and Missy Andrews regarding the importance of the characters in stories:

"All stories are about people . . . Characters are the link between the imaginary world of the author and the reader of his work. It is the strength of the characters, and the author's description of them, that will allow the story to move us, attract us or repel us, give us food for thought, challenge us and affect us."

"Understanding character is a process of identifying the ways in which he is like you, or unlike you; it's a process of finding out how to relate to him, as if he were sitting beside you—because, of course, when you read, he is."
(Adam Andrews 34)

CREATING YOUR OWN CHARACTERS FOR A STORY

All stories have five essential elements: characters, setting, conflict, plot and theme. The job of an author is to "assemble these parts into a beautiful whole." (Andrews 5)

Follow these suggestions to develop your own story plan or to consider when responding to a favorite story you have read.

1. Think of two or more characters you want to use.
2. Decide what role each will play in the story: main character, adversarial character, and/or supporting character.
3. Ask a question to determine what the conflict will be for the main character. What must happen for him to achieve what he wants?
4. Develop each character's personality. Create a set of traits for each character. Plan a particular setting for the story including time, place, and story mood to match your character's needs.
5. Then determine your theme and plot.

DETERMINING CHARACTER ROLES

PRIMARY	OPPOSING	SUPPORTING
central	antagonist	ally
dominant	adversary	assistant
hero	competitor	background
heroine	enemy	companion
leading	foe	participant
main	foil	partner
major	lesser	secondary
principal	opponent	subordinate
protagonist	rival	supporting

ADJECTIVES to Describe Character Traits:

Positive or Neutral   Negative or Neutral

Positive or Neutral		Negative or Neutral	
ambitious	impeccable	arrogant	lonely
authentic	innocent	boisterous	loquacious
colorful	interesting	bumbling	manipulative
comic	loyal	capricious	materialistic
confident	magnanimous	childish	melodramatic
confidential	mature	compulsive	notorious
credible	methodical	contemptible	obnoxious
dedicated	organized	coquettish	raucous
deliberate	patient	depraved	sensuous
distinctive	patriotic	disruptive	shallow
dramatic	pliant	domineering	sinister
eccentric	popular	fraudulent	sordid
eminent	quaint	grandiose	stern
flamboyant	romantic	gullible	stoical
flexible	sensitive	ignorant	tragic
formal	sophisticated	immature	unsavory
idealistic	sporting	impatient	vacillating
illustrious	strong	impulsive	vexatious
imaginative	youthful	infantile	vindictive

The above lists are a sampling of what lies ahead in Section A. Section A lists are arranged by specific character traits with lists of nouns, adjectives, adverbs and verbs for each trait. These words can usually be changed from one part of speech to another by changing the endings.

Character Traits

"[Character is] completely within our control. The poor and the rich, the slow and the smart, the plain and the pretty all have an equal opportunity to become people of character . . . It's determined by choice . . . Our character is never finished. It's constantly shaped and sculpted by the choices we make to nurture or ignore our more noble instincts and to surrender to or overcome negative impulses and corrupting temptations."

From: "That's Just the Way I Am." by Michael Josephson (March 15, 2010)

Introduction to Character Traits

Words for Anger

The Angry Orca

Definition:
    Strong displeasure or wrath toward others

Thoughts on Anger:
    "Anger is a basic human emotion that can be used to your character's advantage or disadvantage. Anger has positive as well as negative value." (Edelstein)

Excerpts from Classical Literature

"Thomas Jefferson once advised us about how to control our temper; when angry, count to ten before you do anything, and when very angry, count to a hundred. Genghis Khan learned the same lesson 800 years ago. His empire stretched from eastern Europe to the Sea of Japan. 'My hawk saved my life!' he cried, 'and how did I repay him? He was my best friend and I have killed him . . . . I have learned a sad lesson today, and that is, never do anything in anger.'"
    The King and His Hawk" Retold by James Baldwin
    Excerpt from: The Children's Book of Virtues by William J. Bennett

"But her voice was thin, had a sound like something thin that would break if you touched it, and he felt bad for not speaking to her. Knowing what he knew, even with the anger, the hot white hate of his anger at her, he still felt bad for not speaking to her, and so to humor her he loosened his belt and pulled the right side out and put the hatchet on and rethreaded the belt."
    From: Hatchet by Gary Paulsen

NOUNS

an annoyance

an argument

the animosity

a 'blowup'

a 'cat fit'

a dispute

exasperation

the fury

an irritation

a quarrel

a 'slow burn'

a 'stew'

a tantrum

a temper

a tiff

NOUNS
Characters

a curmudgeon

a grouch

a grump

a hothead

a Scrooge

10   Character Traits: Anger

ADJECTIVES	ADVERBS	VERBS	ADDITIONAL WORDS
angry	abruptly	bellow	___
antagonistic	aggressively	blow up	___
crabby	angrily	burst	___
displeased	belligerently	chew out	___
enraged	combatively	erupt	___
fiery	contentiously	flame	___
fuming	crossly	growl	___
heated	curtly	holler	___
ill-tempered	destructively	irritate	___
incisive	furiously	lash out	___
infuriated	gruffly	provoke	___
irate	hotly	punish	___
mad	indignantly	rail	___
moody	insanely	rant	___
outraged	loudly	reverberate	___
raging	petulantly	roar	___
ranting	sourly	scream	___
red-hot	sternly	shout	___
seething	tensely	simmer	___
short-tempered	tersely	stomp	___
snarling	uncontrollably	storm	___
storming	unjustly	surge	___
testy	vehemently	upbraid	___
uptight	wrathfully	yell	___

Words for Anger

"My dear brothers, take note of this: everyone should be quick to listen, slow to speak and slow to become angry."

James 1:19 NIV

Words for Cheerfulness

The Cheerful Clownfish

Definition:
    Full of cheer, in good spirits, pleasant, bright

Thoughts on Cheerfulness:
    "Happiness is not created by what happens to us but by our attitude toward each happening."
                       (Anonymous) See Brussell

Excerpts from Classical Literature

Pollyanna has "an overwhelming, unquenchable gladness for everything that has happened or is going to happen. At any rate, her quaint speeches are constantly being repeated to me, and, as near as I can make out, 'just being glad' is the tenor of most of them."
                  From: Pollyanna by Eleanor H. Porter

"'What happened?' I asked the policeman. 'Has somebody taken him?'

'No,' he replied, 'I'm afraid he's been arrested.'

'Arrested? . . . . A dog can't be arrested.'

The policeman threw back his head and laughed. 'I've just been kidding you, Mr. Herriot.'

I laughed too. I didn't mind having the joke played on me because, funny Phelps or not, he was obviously a nice Phelps and would be a kind master for my doggy friend."
        From: "The Market Square Dog" by James Herriot
        Excerpt from: James Herriot's Treasury for Children

NOUNS

her buoyancy
the congeniality
the charm
her cheeriness
the friendliness
the gladness
his joyfulness
the optimism
the solace

NOUNS
Characters

a buddy
a colleague
a dog trainer
an instructor
a nurse
a pal
Pollyanna
a salesman
a stewardess
a teacher
a waitress

12   Character Traits: Cheerfulness

ADJECTIVES	ADVERBS	VERBS	ADDITIONAL WORDS
amenable	agreeably	affirm	
bouncy	amiably	aid	
carefree	blissfully	approach	
cheery	brightly	approve	
congenial	charmingly	arrange	
contented	cheerfully	assist	
delightful	cordially	beam	
easygoing	eagerly	befriend	
friendly	encouragingly	chat	
genial	expectantly	chuckle	
glad	good-naturedly	consent	
good-humored	happily	cooperate	
happy-go-lucky	helpfully	delight	
interested	jokingly	enjoy	
joyful	lightheartedly	giggle	
nice	merrily	greet	
peaceable	mildly	harmonize	
perky	playfully	invite	
satisfied	pleasantly	nurture	
smiling	positively	please	
sociable	satisfactorily	reassure	
sunny	uncomplainingly	suggest	
sweet-tempered	warmly	welcome	
winning	wonderfully	wink	

Words for Cheerfulness

"A cheerful heart is good medicine."
Proverbs 17:22a NIV

Words for Compassion

A Compassionate Dolphin

Definition:
  Deep sympathy for others with a desire to help

Thoughts on Compassion:
  "Mr. Lincoln was remarkably tender of the feelings of others and never wantonly offended even the most despicable, although he was a man of great nerve when aroused."
  (Joseph Gillespie)

Excerpts from Classical Literature

"Yes, I'll go," said the pushmi-pullyu, who saw at once, from the Doctor's face, that he was a man to be trusted. "You have been so kind to the animals here—and the monkeys tell me that I am the only one who will do."
From: The Story of Doctor Dolittle by Hugh Lofting

"And Death gazed and gazed at the Emperor through his great empty eye sockets, and all was still, all was terribly still. And at that moment the loveliest of songs was heard coming in through the window. It was the real nightingale sitting in the branches outside. It had heard of the Emperor's sickness, and so it had come to sing him a song of hope and comfort. And as it sang, the phantom shapes faded away, the blood flowed faster and faster through the Emperor's weak limbs, and Death himself listened and said, 'Go on, go on, little nightingale!'"
From: "The Nightingale" by Hans Christian Andersen
Excerpt from: Elements of Literature edited by Richard Sime

NOUNS
Characters

an advocate

an angel

a benefactor

a child

a do-gooder

a doctor

a donor

a helper

a humanitarian

Good Samaritan

a guardian

a loved one

a mediator

a missionary

a patron

a peacemaker

a priest

a rescuer

a saint

a savior

a soldier

a volunteer

ADJECTIVES	ADVERBS	VERBS	ADDITIONAL WORDS
affectionate	affectionately	bolster	
all heart	bountifully	carry	
caring	comfortingly	cushion	
considerate	compassionately	empathize	
demonstrative	gently	encourage	
exceptional	gracefully	hearten	
forbearing	heartily	hold	
forgiving	hopefully	help	
humane	kindly	identify with	
indulgent	leniently	invigorate	
kindhearted	lovingly	be kind to	
mindful	magnanimously	melt	
neighborly	mercifully	reach out to	
responsive	miraculously	relieve	
sensitive	reassuringly	remedy	
softhearted	responsively	soften	
sympathetic	securely	stir	
tender	selflessly	support	
tenderhearted	softly	sustain	
thoughtful	soothingly	sympathize	
tolerant	sweetly	touch	
understanding	sympathetically	tug at	
warm	tolerantly	understand	
warmhearted	tranquilly	value	

Words for Compassion

"That best portion of a good man's life:
his little, nameless, unremembered acts of kindness and of love."
"Words About Kindness" by William Wordsworth

Words for Complaining

A Complaining Crab

Definition:
Express dissatisfaction, annoyance, or resentment

Thoughts on Complaining:
Complaining comments made by a character can be an important tool of the author's to reveal information to the reader not only about the complainer, but also about the other characters as well.

Excerpts from Classical Literature

"Crying is all right in its way while it lasts. But you have to stop sooner or later, and then you still have to decide what to do."
From: The Silver Chair, Book 6, The Chronicles of Narnia by C.S. Lewis

"'Bah!' said Scrooge. 'Humbug! . . . Merry Christmas, indeed! What reason have you to be merry? You're poor enough.'"
From: A Christmas Carol by Charles Dickens
Excerpt from: The Bookshelf for Boys and Girls

"'Christmas won't be Christmas without any presents,' grumbled Jo, lying on the rug. 'It's so dreadful to be poor!' sighed Meg, looking down at her old dress."
From: Christmas at the Marches [sic], by Louisa May Alcott
Excerpt from: The Bookshelf for Boys and Girls

NOUNS
her bellyaching

the criticism

his dissatisfaction

his gripe

her objection

NOUNS
Characters
a bother

a brat

the crybaby

a fuddy-duddy

a fussbudget

a nuisance

a pessimist

the pest

a rascal

a sourpuss

a teaser

the whiner

the workers

16   Character Traits: Complaining

ADJECTIVES	ADVERBS	VERBS	ADDITIONAL WORDS
argumentative	begrudgingly	accuse	
bad-tempered	blatantly	annoy	
cantankerous	casually	bellyache	
clamoring	continuously	bemoan	
complaining	disagreeably	bother	
cranky	distastefully	deplore	
disgruntled	endlessly	discourage	
dissatisfied	fretfully	fret	
fractious	glumly	frown	
fussy	grudgingly	fume	
grouchy	incessantly	grimace	
grumpy	inconsequentially	gripe	
hard-to-please	inconsiderately	groan	
irritable	irrelevantly	'kick up a fuss'	
out of sorts	negatively	lament	
petty	noisily	murmur	
petulant	nonchalantly	mutter	
quarrelsome	obstinately	nag	
small-minded	offhandedly	pout	
sulking	pathetically	push around	
sullen	peevishly	scowl	
surly	persuasively	sneer	
unhappy	reluctantly	snivel	
unpleasant	rudely	whine	

Words for Complaining

"Do all things without grumbling or disputing..."
Philippians 2:14 NAS

Words for Courage

A Courageous Penguin

Definition:
The ability to face danger or difficulty with bravery

Thoughts on Courage:
When creating courage in your character, be reminded that, "Courage is doing what you are afraid to do. There can be no courage unless you're afraid."
(Edward V. Rickenbacker) See Brussell

Excerpts from Classical Literature

"Afterward, Harriet explained her decision to run the risk of going north alone in these words: 'I had reasoned this out in my mind; there was one of two things I had a <u>right</u> to, liberty or death; if I could not have one, I would have the other; for no man should take me alive; I should fight for my liberty as long as my strength lasted, and when the time came for me to go, the Lord would let them take me.'"
From: Harriet Tubman, A Glory Over Everything by Ann Petry
Excerpt from: Elements of Literature edited by Richard Sime

"Any child in Holland is frightened at the thought of a leak in the dike. Peter understood the danger at once. If the water ran through a little hole it would soon make a larger one and the whole country would be flooded. In a moment he saw what he must do. Throwing away his flowers, he climbed down the side of the dike and thrust his finger into the tiny hole . . . . It grew still colder, and his arm ached, and began to grow stiff and numb . . . . He thought of his brother and sister in their warm beds, and of his dear father and mother. 'I must not let them be drowned,' he thought. 'I must stay here until someone comes, if I have to stay all night.'"
From: The Little Hero of Holland
adapted from Etta Austin Blaisdell and Mary Frances Blaisdell

NOUNS

his boldness
his chivalry
her fearlessness
hardiness
his heroism
the lionhearted
his nerve
her prowess
his valor

NOUNS
Characters

an adventurer
a conqueror
a daredevil
an explorer
a fireman
a knight
a paladin
the pilgrim
a policeman
a soldier
the victor
a warrior

ADJECTIVES	ADVERBS	VERBS	ADDITIONAL WORDS
audacious	admirably	acclaim	___
bold	amazingly	bear	___
brave	bravely	challenge	___
daring	brazenly	climb	___
dauntless	coolly	confront	___
determined	courageously	endeavor	___
gutsy	dispassionately	endure	___
hardy	dramatically	exhibit	___
high-spirited	fearlessly	face	___
indomitable	gallantly	gain	___
invincible	heroically	march	___
manly	mightily	mount	___
nervy	nobly	muster	___
resolute	self-reliantly	overcome	___
Spartan	splendidly	resolve	___
spunky	triumphantly	risk	___
steadfast	unabashedly	rise	___
stouthearted	unfalteringly	stand up to	___
strong	unflinchingly	strain	___
unafraid	unquestioningly	strengthen	___
unconquerable	valiantly	summon	___
undaunted	victoriously	take a chance	___
unswerving	wholeheartedly	venture	___
valorous	wholly	withstand	___

"Be strong and very courageous."
Joshua 1:7a NIV

Words for Criticism

A Critical Carp

Definition:
  Unfavorable comments or judgments of others

Thoughts on Criticism:
  "Criticism, like rain, should be gentle enough to nourish a man's growth without destroying his roots."
  (Frank A. Clark)

Excerpts from Classical Literature

"'Have you ever seen hair like hers? Red as fire! And such shoes,' Bengi continued. 'Can't I borrow one? I'd like to go out rowing and I haven't any boat.' He took hold of one of Pippi's braids but dropped it instantly and cried, 'Ouch, I burned myself.' Then all five boys joined hands around Pippi, jumping up and down and screaming, 'Redhead! Redhead!'"
From: Pippi Longstocking by Astrid Lindgren

"'Done?' snarled the dwarf. 'I haven't done anything, you stupid goose . . . Oh, you idiots!' sputtered the dwarf in a rage. 'You white-faced fools! What good will other mortals do me? There are two too many of you now.'"
From: "Snow White and Rose Red"
Excerpt from: Grimm's Fairy Tales retold by Rose Dobbs

NOUNS
condemnation
the bad press
her disapproval
her evaluation
his faultfinding
the flak
his judgment
the nagging
her objection
the reproach
a swipe

NOUNS Characters
an attack
the coach
the critic
a drill sergeant
the editor
a mudslinger
a nit-picker

20 Character Traits: Criticism

ADJECTIVES	ADVERBS	VERBS	ADDITIONAL WORDS
belittling	abrasively	admonish	
biting	backhandedly	bawl out	
blistering	bitterly	berate	
carping	bluntly	blame	
chafing	brusquely	blast	
coarse	brutally	censure	
critical	caustically	chastise	
cutting	conspicuously	chide	
demanding	cynically	condemn	
demeaning	derisively	crack	
derogatory	disdainfully	declare	
disapproving	disrespectfully	denounce	
discriminating	distressfully	dominate	
faultfinding	frankly	find fault	
harsh	maliciously	'knock'	
hurtful	offensively	put down	
jangling	reproachfully	rebuke	
judgmental	repulsively	reprimand	
nagging	sarcastically	scandalize	
objecting	scornfully	scold	
opinionated	sharply	scrutinize	
saucy	stridently	slam	
severe	surprisingly	slander	
sharp	tauntingly	take down	

Words for Criticism

"Do not judge, and you will not be judged.
Do not condemn, and you will not be condemned."
Luke 6:37 NIV

Words for Curiosity

A Curious Catfish

Definition:

The desire to learn or know, to be inquisitive

Thoughts on Curiosity:

"There are two sorts [of curiosity] . . . one is from interest, which makes us desire to know what may be useful to us; another is from pride, and arises from a desire of knowing what others are ignorant of."

(La Rochefoucauld) See Brussell

Excerpts from Classical Literature

"Mrs. Spencer said I must have asked her a thousand questions already. I suppose I had, too, but how are you going to find out about things if you don't ask questions? And what <u>does</u> make the roads red? . . . . Well, that is one of the things to find out sometime. Isn't it splendid to think of all the things there are to find out about? It just makes me feel glad to be alive—it's such an interesting world."

From: Anne of Green Gables by L.M. Montgomery

"Ralph was tired after a night of such great excitement and full of dreams. Now that he had seen the hall he could no longer be satisfied with room 215. It was not enough. He longed to see the rest of the world—the dining room and the kitchen and the storeroom and the garbage cans out back. He wanted to see the game room . . . . He wanted to go outdoors and brave the owls to hunt for seeds. Ralph, a growing mouse who needed his rest, dozed off . . . beside the motorcycle."

From: The Mouse and The Motorcycle by Beverly Cleary

NOUNS

her inquisitiveness

his meddling

the search

the study

NOUNS

Characters

an artist

our creator

an eccentric

an experimenter

an inspector

the inventor

an investigator

an originator

the pathfinder

a pioneer

the poet

the researcher

a scientist

a seeker

a tourist

a traveler

22   Character Traits: Curiosity

ADJECTIVES	ADVERBS	VERBS	ADDITIONAL WORDS
advancing	adventurously	awaken	
analytical	artfully	comb	
artistic	astonishingly	develop	
curious	creatively	discover	
fascinating	imaginatively	display	
forward	incredulously	envision	
ingenious	inexplicably	evaluate	
innovative	inquisitively	examine	
intriguing	insatiably	experience	
inventive	interestingly	explore	
novel	intrusively	ferret out	
original	magnificently	inquire	
precocious	mysteriously	inspect	
prowling	peculiarly	interfere	
prying	picturesquely	investigate	
remarkable	questioningly	marvel	
scrutinizing	quizzically	probe	
searching	reflectively	prompt	
seeking	resourcefully	pursue	
snooping	speculatively	puzzle over	
snoopy	strangely	query	
stimulating	unusually	quest	
unique	urgently	question	
unprecedented	wonderingly	sniff out	

Words for Curiosity

"Curiosity is one of the permanent and certain characteristics of a vigorous intellect."
(Dr. Samuel Johnson)

Words for Dishonesty

A Dishonest Devil Ray

Definition:
> A disposition to lie, cheat, or steal

Thoughts on Dishonesty:
> When developing a character who lies be sure to show this trait through his actions, his speech, and others' observations rather than tell the reader that he is dishonest. Deceit is "the smiler with the knife under the cloak."
> (Geoffrey Chaucer) See Brussell

Excerpts from Classical Literature

"Tom lay thinking. Presently it occurred to him that he wished he was sick; then he could stay home from school . . . . So he fell to groaning with considerable spirit . . . . Tom was suffering in reality, now, so handsomely was his imagination working, and so his groans had gathered quite a genuine tone.

'So all this row was because you thought you'd get to stay home from school and go a-fishing? Tom, Tom, I love you so, and you seem to try every way you can to break my old heart with your outrageousness.'"

From: The Adventures of Tom Sawyer by Mark Twain
Excerpt from: Elements of Literature by Holt, Rinehart, and Winston

"One day two swindlers came. They claimed they were weavers and said they could weave the finest cloth imaginable . . . but the clothes made of this material possessed the wonderful quality of being invisible to any man who was unfit for his office, or who was hopelessly stupid."

From: "The Emperor's New Clothes" by Hans Christian Andersen
Excerpt from: Elements of Literature by Holt, Rinehart, and Winston

NOUNS

her deceit
the falsity
his fraud
a hoax
a rip-off
the trickery
a white lie
a whopper
a yarn

NOUNS
Characters

a blackmailer
a charlatan
the cheater
a chiseler
a con artist
the crook
impersonator
an imposter
a knave
the racketeer
a sneak
a thief

24 Character Traits: Dishonesty

ADJECTIVES	ADVERBS	VERBS	ADDITIONAL WORDS
bluffing	ambiguously	circumvent	_____
cheating	beguilingly	concoct	_____
counterfeit	craftily	defraud	_____
corrupt	cunningly	duck	_____
crooked	deceptively	dupe	_____
deceitful	deviously	falsify	_____
double-crossing	dishonestly	fool	_____
double-dealing	disingenuously	hoodwink	_____
elusive	fallaciously	lie	_____
evasive	fraudulently	lure	_____
false	hypocritically	make up	_____
fibbing	insincerely	misrepresent	_____
lying	misleadingly	pretend	_____
scheming	shrewdly	scam	_____
shady	slickly	setup	_____
shifty	slyly	slant	_____
slippery	spuriously	snooker	_____
sneaky	strategically	snow	_____
stealing	surreptitiously	stretch the truth	_____
thieving	suspiciously	swindle	_____
tricky	tentatively	switch	_____
underhanded	treacherously	tell a tall tale	_____
untrustworthy	unfairly	twist	_____
untruthful	unreliably		_____

Words for Dishonesty

". . . whoever is dishonest with very little will also be dishonest with much. So if you have not been trustworthy in handling worldly wealth, who will trust you with true riches?"
Luke 16:10b, 11 NIV

Words for Envy

An Envious Eel

Definitions:
    Wanting what someone else has

Thoughts on Envy:

Envy is "a thousand eyes, but none with correct vision."
(Isacher Hurwitz)

"If you have a longing desire to possess the goods which you have not, though you may say you would not possess them unjustly, you are . . . covetous."
(Saint Francis de Sales) See Brussell

Excerpts from Classical Literature

"[The Wicked Prince] had built this city, which was called Vanity Fair, just beyond the Dark Valley and the wilderness, because he knew that when the pilgrims reached its gates they would be feeling tired and faint, and he hoped that it would then be easy to persuade them to stay there, instead of going farther on the Way of the King.

So he filled the great city with everything that was pleasant and beautiful. It had broad streets and handsome houses, and the stalls in its market were covered with glittering wares. All day long the people were passing busily up and down. They wore fine clothes and spent their whole time in pleasing themselves, and the Wicked Prince took care to give them plenty of things to enjoy so that they might never have a moment to spare in which to think of the King whom they had forsaken."

From: Little Pilgrim's Progress, by Helen L. Taylor
Excerpt from Pilgrim's Progress by John Bunyan

NOUNS

an appetite
the burning
his craving
her desire
his grudge
the hunger
the ill will
his need
an obsession
one-track mind
a penchant
a pipe dream
her resentment
the rivalry
her sighing
his temptation
her unhappiness
her yearning

NOUNS
Characters

a debauchee
an epicure
a hedonist

ADJECTIVES	ADVERBS	VERBS	ADDITIONAL WORDS
aching	compulsively	ache	
agog	discontentedly	agonize	
bitter	enticingly	begrudge	
consuming	fervently	burn	
dissatisfied	fervidly	covet	
envious	feverishly	crave	
gluttonous	greedily	desire	
grabby	hungrily	devour	
grasping	impulsively	expect	
green	indulgingly	hanker	
green-eyed	intensely	hunger	
hoggish	inwardly	idolize	
insatiable	lavishly	itch for	
jealous	longingly	lament	
malevolent	lustfully	languish	
obsessive	mockingly	need	
omnivorous	obviously	object	
piggish	openly	pine	
possessive	ravenously	prize	
thirsty	resentfully	regret	
unquenchable	selfishly	resent	
voracious	spitefully	want	
wolfish	wishfully	yearn	

Words for Envy

"Let us not become boastful, challenging one another, envying one another."
Galatians 5:26 NAS

Words for Exuberance

An Exuberant Sea Otter

Definition:
Being uninhibitedly enthusiastic or vigorous

Thoughts on Exuberance:
"Every great and commanding moment in the annals of the world is the triumph of some enthusiasm."
(Ralph Waldo Emerson) See Brussell

"The most beautiful word on earth."
(Christian Morgenstern)

Excerpts from Classical Literature

"Whenever he went dodging about the village, he was surrounded by a troop of them [children], hanging on his skirts, clambering on his back, and playing a thousand tricks on him with impunity. . ."
From: "Rip Van Winkle" by Washington Irving
Excerpt from: The Bookshelf for Boys and Girls

"I used to run with them [the older colts], and had great fun. We used to gallop all together round the field, as hard as we could go. Sometimes the play was rough, for they would frequently bite and kick, as well as gallop."
From: Adventures of Black Beauty, by Anna Sewell

"Anyway, having set my clock-radio, I woke up to all the tweeting and brass band from the Kwai movie the next morning, and I got out of bed quicker than on most weekends . . . Suddenly I realized I wasn't walking—I was strutting . . . I'd never felt so good. So confident. So beautiful."
From: The Trouble With Tuck by Theodore Taylor

NOUNS

his amusement
the laughter
the merriment
her zeal

NOUNS
Characters

an actor
the children
a clown
a comedian
a contestant
a dancer
an entertainer
the gymnasts
a humorist
the jester
the kittens
a performance
a puppy
the sea otter
a speaker
a winner

ADJECTIVES	ADVERBS	VERBS	ADDITIONAL WORDS
adventurous	amicably	affect	_____
affable	ardently	astonish	_____
animated	contagiously	bounce	_____
assertive	emotionally	burst	_____
brash	engagingly	celebrate	_____
bubbly	enthusiastically	dance	_____
buoyant	excitedly	enliven	_____
dynamic	expressively	entertain	_____
energetic	flippantly	exclaim	_____
extroverted	gleefully	gush	_____
exuberant	hilariously	impress	_____
fun-loving	impetuously	inspire	_____
gregarious	joyfully	kick up his heels	_____
high-spirited	joyously	laugh	_____
jolly	overzealously	lavish	_____
jubilant	passionately	perform	_____
lively	profusely	play	_____
merry	quickly	radiate	_____
on-the-move	rapidly	rejoice	_____
outgoing	spontaneously	revel	_____
spirited	sprightly	sparkle	_____
talkative	swiftly	sprint	_____
vigorous	vivaciously	thrill	_____
vivacious	whimsically	whirl	_____

Words for Exuberance

"Life is tons of discipline. Your first discipline is your vocabulary; then your grammar and your punctuation. Then, in your exuberance and bounding energy you say you're going to add to that. Then you add rhyme and meter. And your delight is in that power."

(Robert Frost)

Words for Fearfulness

A Fearful Flounder

Definition:
  A painful emotion due to expecting danger or evil

Thoughts on Fearfulness:

"The only thing we have to fear is fear itself."
  (Franklin D. Roosevelt)

"A slinking cat I find beneath the lilacs of my mind."
  (Sophie Tunnell) See Brussell

Excerpts from Classical Literature

"There was a snarl, and a big raccoon I've never seen walked past him, growling and looking ferocious. Jessie C. stood motionless—I might say, scared stiff."
  From: My Side of the Mountain, by Jean Craighead George

"The flopping salmon slapped against the sleeping Ribsy. Ribsy woke up, saw the strange flopping thing, gave one terrified yelp, and tried to scramble away from it . . . . Again, it slapped against Ribsy, who fell over the lunch boxes in his struggle to get away."
  From: Henry and Ribsy by Beverly Cleary

"The forest below them was wildly tangled and dark. Tom and Uncle Nick had never seen such a scary, overgrown, wild place. Every now and then Tom had a glimpse of running water through the trees."
  From: The Littles and Their Amazing New Friend by John Peterson and Roberta Carter Clark

NOUNS

her alarm
apprehension
consternation
his dismay
her panic
a scare
the terror

NOUNS
Characters

a chicken
a coward
a creampuff
a deserter
a 'fraidy-cat
a mouse
a paper tiger
a patsy
a pawn
a pushover
a quitter
a runaway
a weakling
a wimp

30 Character Traits: Fearfulness

ADJECTIVES	ADVERBS	VERBS	ADDITIONAL WORDS
abject	anxiously	avoid	
afraid	apprehensively	banish	
chickenhearted	basely	beg	
cowering	embarrassingly	confess	
debilitated	faintly	cringe	
fainthearted	falteringly	crouch	
faithless	feebly	dread	
fearful	frantically	draw back	
frightened	gutlessly	feign	
jittery	helplessly	flee	
mousy	hesitantly	flinch	
panicky	hopelessly	grovel	
petrified	limply	hide	
scared	miserably	quiver	
shrinking	nervously	run	
skittish	pathetically	recoil	
spineless	pityingly	shame	
subservient	powerlessly	shy away	
suspicious	shamefully	shift	
timid	tremulously	shake	
trembling	uncertainly	shrink back	
wavering	unsteadily	shudder	
weak-kneed	unsurely	slither	
yellow bellied	weakly	wince	

Words for Fearfulness

"He who is not everyday conquering some fear has not learned the secret of life."
(Ralph Waldo Emerson)

Words for Generosity

A Generous Manatee

Definition:
    Freely giving or sharing something of value

Thoughts on Generosity:
"To be rich in admiration and free from envy, to rejoice greatly in the good of others, to love with such generosity of heart that your love is still a dear possession in absence or unkindness—these are the gifts which money cannot buy."   (Robert Louis Stevenson)

Excerpts from Classical Literature

"Harriet wanted to pay this woman who had befriended her. But she had no money. She gave her the patchwork quilt, the only beautiful object she had ever owned."
From: Harriet Tubman, A Glory Over Everything by Ann Petry

"'I can't . . .' the Rainbow Fish started to say . . . . 'Give away my scales? My beautiful shining scales? Never. How could I ever be happy without them?'

Everyone wanted a glittering scale. The Rainbow Fish shared his scales left and right. And the more he gave away, the more delighted he became. When the water around him filled with glimmering scales, he at last felt at home among the other fish . . . . Finally the Rainbow Fish had only one shining scale left. His most prized possessions had been given away, yet he was very happy."
From: The Rainbow Fish by Marcus Pfister

NOUNS
the alms
his altruism
her donation
the endowment
his generosity
his selflessness
her service
the sharing
her unselfishness

NOUNS
Characters
the backer
the benefactor
the charity
the church
a contributor
a fundraiser
a giver
a grantor
the patron
philanthropist
a sponsor
a supporter

ADJECTIVES	ADVERBS	VERBS	ADDITIONAL WORDS
ample	abundantly	award	
beneficial	accommodatingly	bequeath	
benevolent	altruistically	bestow	
big-hearted	bounteously	bless	
charitable	copiously	confer	
effusive	entirely	contribute	
exorbitant	freely	deliver	
expansive	frivolously	dispense	
extravagant	fruitfully	donate	
free-flowing	fully	endow	
freehanded	greatly	favor	
generous	liberally	furnish	
giving	lushly	gave	
hospitable	munificently	grant	
humanitarian	outlandishly	hand	
large	productively	impart	
magnanimous	prolifically	increase	
openhanded	readily	invest	
outpouring	richly	multiply	
overflowing	sacrificially	offer	
philanthropic	substantially	present	
plenteous	sufficiently	provide	
plentiful	unreservedly	shower	
unselfish	unselfishly	transfer	

Words for Generosity

"A generous man will himself be blessed..."
Proverbs 22:9a NIV

Character Traits: Generosity

Words for Gossip

A Gossipy Octopus

Definition:
    Idle talk, rumors about other people, usually who are not present

Thoughts on Gossip:
    "The art of saying nothing in a way that leaves practically nothing unsaid."
        (Walter Winchell) See Brussell

    "The lengthening of the tongue to hammer-like proportions."
        (Anonymous) See Brussell

Excerpts from Classical Literature

"Maddie blinked away the tears that came every time she thought of Wanda standing alone in that sunny spot in the schoolyard, looking stolidly over at the group of laughing girls after she had walked off, after she had said, 'Sure, a hundred of them, all lined up.'"
    From: "The Hundred Dresses" by Eleanor Estes
    Excerpt from: Seventy Favorite Stories for Young Readers

"'Well, today she was so mad at her father that she told her so-called friends Wilma and Bobby Sue about it.'

'Yeah?'

'And those two—two—' She looked for a word vile enough to describe Janice Avery's friends and found none. 'Those two girls blabbed it all over the seventh grade.'"
    From: Bridge to Terabithia by Katherine Paterson

NOUNS

an earful
the grapevine
the hearsay
her prattle
the report
a rumor
the scandal
the scoop
a tidbit

NOUNS Characters

blabbermouth
the busybody
a chatterbox
a gossiper
a jabberer
the meddler
the mudslinger
the snoop
a talebearer
a tattletale
the whisperer

Character Traits: Gossip

ADJECTIVES	ADVERBS	VERBS	ADDITIONAL WORDS
backbiting	desperately	circulate	
blabbing	disgracefully	defame	
blurting	dishonorably	divulge	
buzzing	disparagingly	expose	
chattering	distastefully	get an earful	
chilling	doubtfully	give away	
degrading	furtively	hint	
disgusting	idly	imply	
gossipy	ignorantly	insinuate	
groundless	inconceivably	jabber	
hushed	jeeringly	let out	
idle talking	libelously	let slip	
impolite	outrageously	parrot	
jabbering	privately	prattle	
juicy	pryingly	pry	
rotten	regrettably	reveal	
stinging	scandalously	shock	
tactless	secretly	slur	
tale-bearing	shockingly	spill the beans	
tale-telling	slanderously	spread rumors	
tasty	thoughtlessly	stick his nose into	
terrible	underhandedly	tattle	
unflattering	unfavorably	uncover	
whispering	untruthfully	unveil	

Words for Gossip

"He gossips habitually; he lacks the common wisdom to keep still that deadly enemy of man, his own tongue."
(Mark Twain)

Words for Honor

An Honorable Sea Horse

Definition:
Being held in high public esteem, respect
A keen sense of right and wrong

Thoughts on Honor:
"Our own heart, and not other men's opinions form our true honor."
(Samuel Taylor Coleridge)

"A man has honor if he holds himself to an ideal of conduct though it is inconvenient, unprofitable, or dangerous to do so."
(Walter Lippmann)

Excerpts from Classical Literature

"His greatest mission was to accomplish two things: first, to save his country from dismemberment and ruin; and second, to free his country from the great crime of slavery . . . . Taking him for all in all, measuring the tremendous magnitude of the work before him, considering the necessary means to ends, and surveying the end from the beginning, infinite wisdom has seldom sent any man into the world better fitted for his mission than Abraham Lincoln."

From: "The Mysterious Mr. Lincoln" by Russell Freedman
Excerpt from: Elements of Literature edited by Richard Sime

"O Captain! my Captain! rise up and hear the bells; Rise up—for you the flag is flung—for you the bugle trills, For you bouquets and ribbon'd wreaths—for you the shores a-crowding, For you they call, the swaying mass, their eager faces turning."

From: "O Captain! My Captain!" by Walt Whitman
Excerpt from: Poetry for Young People: Walt Whitman

NOUNS

the approval
his candor
the esteem
her fairness
the gospel
his integrity
her loyalty
the openness
the praise
the respect
righteousness
her reputation
the truthfulness
his valor

NOUNS
Characters

a herald
the judge
a king
an official
the president
a prophet
a referee

36   Character Traits: Honor

ADJECTIVES	ADVERBS	VERBS	ADDITIONAL WORDS
acclaimed	adoringly	admire	
chivalrous	commendably	applaud	
conscientious	decently	appreciate	
dependable	distinctively	cherish	
dignified	excellently	compliment	
distinguished	fairly	consider	
esteemed	favorably	decorate	
ethical	gloriously	devote	
exemplary	highly	hold dear	
faithful	incomparably	laud	
honest	invaluably	look up to	
honorable	irreproachably	love	
just	morally	magnify	
knightly	outstandingly	praise	
noble	prestigiously	prize	
notable	pricelessly	recognize	
of good repute	purely	regard	
reliable	reputably	respect	
respectable	reverently	revere	
righteous	righteously	salute	
sincere	strikingly	treasure	
trustworthy	superbly	uphold	
truthful	supremely	value	
virtuous	trustingly	worship	

Words for Honor

"It is to a man's honor to avoid strife, but every fool is quick to quarrel."
Proverbs 20:3 NIV

Words for Hostility

The Hostile Shark

Definition:
Antagonistic, not friendly, opposing

Thoughts on Hostility:

"It is my most ardent desire, not only to soften the inevitable calamities of war, but even to introduce on every occasion as great a share of tenderness and humanity, as can possibly be exercised in a state of hostility."
(George Washington)

"Constant kindness can accomplish much. As the sun makes ice melt, kindness causes misunderstanding, mistrust, and hostility to evaporate."
(Albert Schweitzer)

Excerpts from Classical Literature

"The Grinch hated Christmas! The whole Christmas season! Now, please don't ask why. No one quite knows the reason . . . . But I think that the most likely reason of all may have been that his heart was two sizes too small."
From: How the Grinch Stole Christmas by Dr. Seuss

"Spitz never lost an opportunity of showing his teeth. He even went out of his way to bully Buck, striving constantly to start the fight which could end only in the death of one or the other."
From: The Call of the Wild by Jack London

"I shall never forget my next master. He had black eyes and a hooked nose, and his voice was as harsh as the grinding of cart wheels over gravel stones . . . . He was hard on the men, and the men were hard on the horses."
From: Black Beauty by Anna Sewell

NOUNS
his antagonism
his battle
his bitterness
her contempt
his defiance
the enmity
the hatred
his infamy
her malice
the war
the wrath

NOUNS Characters
the antagonist
a bad guy
a bandit
a competitor
an enemy
his foe
an opponent
the rebel
a traitor
a villain

Character Traits: Hostility

ADJECTIVES	ADVERBS	VERBS	ADDITIONAL WORDS
adverse	accusingly	abuse	_____
aggressive	adversely	attack	_____
anti	callously	batter	_____
avenging	chillingly	blare	_____
brutal	cruelly	blister	_____
cold	dangerously	coerce	_____
combative	darkly	deny	_____
competitive	extremely	destroy	_____
enraged	ferociously	dictate	_____
explosive	frightfully	disrupt	_____
fierce	harshly	eliminate	_____
fighting	hatefully	explode	_____
hardened	heartlessly	flare	_____
malicious	hostilely	hurl	_____
mean	mercilessly	inflict	_____
militant	powerfully	order	_____
nasty	ruthlessly	overwhelm	_____
opposing	savagely	pulverize	_____
retaliating	unfortunately	rage	_____
seething	vengefully	rampage	_____
spiteful	venomously	shriek	_____
treacherous	viciously	thunder	_____
viperous	violently	whip	_____
warlike	wickedly	wreck	_____

Words for Hostility

"People who fly into a rage always make a bad landing."
(Will Rogers)

Character Traits: Hostility

Words for Humility

A Humble Oyster

Definition:
    Having a modest opinion of one's own importance

Thoughts on Humility:

> "Pride juggles with her toppling towers,
> They strike the sun and cease,
> But the firm feet of humility
> They grip the ground like trees."
> From: The Ballad of the White Horse by G.K. Chesterton

> "Sense shines with a double luster when it is set in humility. An able yet humble man is a jewel worth a kingdom."
> (William Penn)

Excerpts from Classical Literature

"It [the barn] often had a sort of peaceful smell, as though nothing bad could happen ever again in the world . . . . Here she [Fern] sat quietly during the long afternoons thinking and listening and watching Wilbur."
From: Charlotte's Web, by E.B. White

"A person is a person, no matter how small."
From: Horton Hears a Who by Dr. Seuss

"If you compare yourself with others, you may become vain or bitter, for always there will be greater and lesser persons than yourself. Enjoy your achievements as well as your plans. Keep interested in your own career, however humble; it is a real possession in the changing fortunes of time."
From: Desiderata by Max Ehrmann

NOUNS

- her blissfulness
- his calmness
- a contentment
- forbearance
- his godliness
- the mildness
- her modesty
- peacefulness
- his pleasantness
- the quietness
- a restfulness
- reverence
- a serenity
- her servility
- a stillness
- subjection
- the tranquility
- unobtrusiveness

NOUNS
Characters

- Abraham Lincoln
- Gandhi
- Mother Teresa

Character Traits: Humility

ADJECTIVES	ADVERBS	VERBS	ADDITIONAL WORDS
bashful	blamelessly	abide	
blushing	calmly	acknowledge	
courteous	conservatively	appease	
demure	discreetly	calm	
gentle	graciously	comfort	
kind	humbly	defer	
meek	innocently	ease	
mellow	moderately	indulge	
mild	modestly	lighten	
moderate	naturally	negotiate	
modest	peacefully	pacify	
polite	quietly	pause	
receptive	reasonably	placate	
reserved	serenely	quell	
respectful	silently	quiet	
restrained	simply	react	
retiring	sincerely	reconcile	
reverential	tactfully	remain	
simple	temperately	satisfy	
soft-spoken	timidly	soothe	
subdued	unobtrusively	sweeten	
unassertive	unpretentiously	temper	
unassuming	virtuously	wait	
unobtrusive	wholesomely	win over	

Words for Humility

"Better to be lowly in spirit and among the oppressed than to share plunder with the proud."

Proverbs 16:19 NIV

Character Traits: Humility 41

Words for Lawlessness

A Lawless Lobster

Definition:
    Without laws, outside the law, having no rules

Thoughts on Lawlessness:

"People who are honest, kind, and fair only when there is something to gain shouldn't be confused with people of real character who demonstrate these qualities habitually, under all circumstances. Character is not a fancy coat we put on for show; it's who we really are."

(Michael Josephson)

Excerpts from Classical Literature

"'They're not going to make it!' Dr. Henderson cried, shaking her head.

'Look!' said Mobutu. I see His Excellency!' They searched in the direction Mobutu was pointing and finally spotted one tiny figure standing defiantly in the path of the Stone, one hand outstretched to point a silver saber, the other hand a shaking fist. Mobutu shook his head in sorrow and wonder. 'He still defies the Stone! He defies the God of the Motosas!'"

From: The Secret of the Desert Stone by Frank Peretti

"Olaf continued to gaze downward, and the Baudelaires could not tell if he looked pleased or disappointed. 'Thanks to you orphans,' he said, 'it's too late to destroy everyone with the Medusoid Mycelium, but at least we got to start a fire.'"

From: Penultimate Peril: A Series of Unfortunate Events Book the Twelfth by Lemony Snicket

NOUNS

the anarchy
the chaos
destructiveness
the disorder
the terrorism
the tyranny
the unrest
an uprising

NOUNS Characters

an agitator
a bully
a clamor
a criminal
a delinquent
a despot
the mutineer
an outlaw
a revolutionary
the ruffian
a tormentor
a troublemaker
a tyrant

Character Traits: Lawlessness

ADJECTIVES	ADVERBS	VERBS	ADDITIONAL WORDS
brazen	chaotically	break the rules	
contrary	coercively	cover up	
defiant	contemptuously	decline	
disobedient	defiantly	desert	
disorderly	drastically	destroy	
headstrong	evasively	differ	
insubordinate	forcefully	disagree	
lawless	forcibly	disobey	
naughty	insidiously	evade	
noncompliant	involuntarily	flout	
rash	menacingly	forge	
raucous	perilously	misbehave	
rebellious	provocatively	mutiny	
remiss	rashly	neglect	
resistive	rebelliously	oppose	
rowdy	recklessly	overthrow	
uncontrolled	rigidly	rebel	
undisciplined	roughly	revolt	
ungovernable	spitefully	riot	
unmanageable	terrifyingly	rise up	
unruly	threateningly	scorn	
villainous	unscrupulously	steal	
wayward	unsparingly	thwart	
willful	wildly	violate	

Words for Lawlessness

"Lawless are they that make their wills their law."
(William Shakespeare)

Words for Laziness

A Lazy Lionfish

Definition:
    Not eager or willing to work or exert oneself

Thoughts on Laziness:
    "How soon *not now* becomes *never*."
        (Martin Luther)

    "Laziness travels so slowly that poverty soon overtakes him."
        (Benjamin Franklin)

Excerpts from Classical Literature

"Best of all she liked big boxes. So she was happy indeed one sleepy summer day—when even her sometimes-friend Fats Watson was out of town—to see a truck deliver a great, tall box."
From: *Christina Katerina and the Box* by Patricia Lee Gauch

"It was May, and the day was warm and humid. Most of the band were scattered through the forest on one mission or another. A few men lay lazily in the shade of the green wood tree with Robin."
From: *Robin Hood* by Howard Pyle

"The little cat was sitting very upright on the thick rug which lay in front of the fireplace in which the coals glowed and flamed. The three Bassets were already lying there but they seemed used to Debbie because two of them sniffed her in a bored manner and the third merely cocked a sleepy eye at her before flopping back to sleep."
From: *The Christmas Day Kitten* by James Herriot

NOUNS
her detachment
his disregard
her indolence
the laxness
his lethargy
neglectfulness
the torpor
her unconcern
worthlessness

NOUNS
Characters
a bum
a dawdler
a dullard
the goof-off
the idler
the laggard
the lazybones
a plodder
a slacker
a sluggard

44   Character Traits: Laziness

ADJECTIVES	ADVERBS	VERBS	ADDITIONAL WORDS
blah	absentmindedly	bore	
boring	apathetically	bother	
careless	blankly	burn out	
colorless	carelessly	dillydally	
disinterested	dully	dream	
drab	flatly	drift	
dreary	halfheartedly	drowse	
ho hum	inattentively	expend	
idle	lazily	fritter	
inactive	lethargically	irk	
indifferent	lifelessly	irritate	
irresponsible	listlessly	loiter	
lackadaisical	monotonously	loll	
laid back	passively	lounge	
loafing	pointlessly	malinger	
procrastinating	slothfully	pass the time	
repetitious	sluggishly	shirk	
shiftless	tediously	sprawl	
slack	unemotionally	stall	
spiritless	unenthusiastically	vegetate	
stale	unimaginatively	vex	
tiresome	unresponsively	go to sleep	
unenergetic	unthinkingly	wear out	
uninteresting	vacantly	yawn	

Words for Laziness

"Laziness may appear attractive, but work gives satisfaction."
(Anne Frank)

Words for Obedience

An Obedient Dogfish

Definition:
   Responding quickly and willingly to directions

Thoughts on Obedience:

"Wicked men obey for fear, but the good for love."
(Aristotle)

"I have thought about it a great deal, and the more I think, the more certain I am that obedience is the gateway through which knowledge, yes, and love, too, enter the mind of the child."
(Anne Sullivan)

Excerpts from Classical Literature

"'All I need is . . .' she started to say. She choked back the lump in her throat and screwed up her courage. 'Could I have a bit of earth?' she asked . . . 'May I take it from anywhere?' she went on. 'As long as it's not wanted?'. . . Her heart was soaring. Lord Craven had said she could have a bit of earth! That meant he gave her permission to tend the secret garden! He had said she could take the land from anywhere, hadn't he? As long as it was a place that wasn't wanted? Mary knew for certain that Lord Craven didn't want the secret garden. After all, he'd ordered it locked."
From: The Secret Garden, a novelization by M.J. Carr

NOUNS

his allegiance
her compliance
his deference
her passivity
respectfulness
her submission

NOUNS
Characters

an assistant
the children
a citizen
the conformist
a crew
a member
a novice
the participant
a pet
her servant
the subject
a team player
the troop

46   Character Traits: Obedience

ADJECTIVES	ADVERBS	VERBS	ADDITIONAL WORDS
accepting	absolutely	abide by	_____
acknowledging	astutely	accept	_____
acquiescent	compellingly	act upon	_____
agreeable	consciously	agree	_____
allowing	correctly	allow	_____
assenting	deliberately	answer to	_____
attentive	easily	attempt to	_____
compliant	independently	bow to	_____
controllable	loyally	carry out	_____
devoted	mutually	comply	_____
docile	obediently	concur	_____
dutiful	predictably	discharge	_____
easy	properly	follow	_____
law-abiding	regularly	fulfill	_____
manageable	reliably	heed	_____
obliging	responsibly	keep	_____
submissive	rightly	knuckle under	_____
tame	sensibly	live by	_____
teachable	seriously	mind	_____
under control	somberly	respond	_____
well-behaved	strictly	submit	_____
well-trained	totally	surrender	_____
willing	undoubtedly	is loyal to	_____
yielding	voluntarily	is ruled by	_____

Words for Obedience

"Justice is the insurance which we have on our lives and property. Obedience is the premium which we pay for it."

(William Penn)

Words for Pride

A Prideful Puffer Fish

Definition:
A high opinion of one's own or another's importance

Thoughts on Pride:
"A proud man is always looking down on things and people; and, of course, as long as you're looking down, you can't see something that's above you." (C.S. Lewis)

Excerpts from Classical Literature

"He was a magnificent creature, huge and proudly built. Donald saw the gloss of the black coat and the great curving muscles of the strong legs, the massive hoofs, the powerful arch of the neck, the proud crest of the head. Donald imagined he could see the flash of black intelligent eyes. Surely, a nobler creature never roamed the plains!"

From: "The Black Stallion and the Red Mare" by Gladys F. Lewis
Excerpt from: Seventy Favorite Stories for Young Readers

"'From the first moment I saw you,' she went on, 'I hated your arrogance, your conceit and your insensitivity to others. I felt that you were the last man in the world I would ever marry!'. . . . Suddenly, Elizabeth felt ashamed of herself. Darcy was prideful, but she had been prejudiced! . . . . 'I who pride myself on intelligence. I have courted prejudice and ignorance.'"

From: Pride and Prejudice by Jane Austen

NOUNS
her aloofness
his arrogance
her bravado
her distain
his ego
his haughtiness
the presumption
the vanity

NOUNS
Characters
a big mouth
a big talker
a boaster
the braggart
a grandstander
a hotshot
a know-it-all
a peacock
a show-off
a snob
a windbag

48   Character Traits: Pride

ADJECTIVES	ADVERBS	VERBS	ADDITIONAL WORDS
aloof	amateurishly	bluster	
cocky	arrogantly	boast	
conceited	confidently	bombard	
cool	excessively	brag	
domineering	extensively	claim	
egotistical	extravagantly	congratulate	
haughty	fabulously	crow	
high and mighty	flagrantly	draw attention	
huffy	flamboyantly	exaggerate	
inflated	frequently	exult	
insolent	inappropriately	fake	
lofty	increasingly	flaunt	
narcissistic	irresistibly	flourish	
overbearing	irresponsibly	gloat	
overblown	ornately	proclaim	
prideful	overconfidently	profess	
puffed-up	pompously	rave	
self-centered	presumptuously	show off	
self-satisfied	pretentiously	sound off	
snobbish	repetitively	strut	
stuck-up	smugly	swagger	
superior	unceasingly	talk big	
vain	vaingloriously	trumpet	
well-pleased	willfully	vaunt	

Words for Pride

"Pride goes before destruction. . ."
Proverbs 16:18a NIV

Words for Responsibility

A Responsible Sea Turtle

Definition:
> To be accountable, able to make decisions

Thoughts on Responsibility:
> "Work to carry on within, duties to perform abroad, influences to exert which are peculiarly ours, and which no conscience but our own can teach."
> (Adapted from William Ellery Channing) See Brussell

Excerpts from Classical Literature

"The winter was half over before I finished the house, but I slept there every night and felt secure because of the strong fence. The foxes came when I was cooking my food and stood outside gazing through the cracks, and the wild dogs also came, gnawing at the whale ribs, growling because they could not get in."
From: Island of the Blue Dolphins by Scott O'Dell

"That was the first night of my new duties, and in the course of the next day I had got well into the run of them. I had to serve at the meals, which the captain took at regular hours, sitting down with the officer who was off duty; all the day through I would be running with a dram to one or the other of my three masters; and at night I slept on a blanket thrown on the deck boards at the aftermost end of one of the roundhouses."
From: Kidnapped by Robert Louis Stevenson

NOUNS
accountability
his authority
the credence
dependability
her duty
her obligation
reliability
her trust

NOUNS Characters
the captain
a chief
a commander
the diplomat
a director
his disciple
the leader
a manager
an officer
the ruler
a trustee

Character Traits: Responsibility

ADJECTIVES	ADVERBS	VERBS	ADDITIONAL WORDS
active	ably	apply	
adept	aptly	attend to	
busy	attentively	care for	
capable	carefully	concentrate	
concerted	competently	determine	
diligent	conscientiously	develop	
efficient	constantly	establish	
engaged	devotedly	exercise	
enterprising	directly	exert	
experienced	earnestly	hustle	
hard-working	effectively	intend	
intense	faithfully	labor	
intent	habitually	motivate	
levelheaded	industriously	occupy	
persevering	painstakingly	persist	
prompt	patiently	plug away	
qualified	persistently	prepare	
responsible	practically	produce	
skillful	proficiently	show	
steady	studiously	stabilize	
thorough	systematically	study	
tireless	unendingly	toil	
upright	validly	travail	
veteran	zealously	work	

Words for Responsibility

"I know your deeds, your hard work and your perseverance . . . You have persevered and have endured hardships . . . and have not grown weary."

Revelation 2:2a, 3 NIV

Words for Stubbornness

A Stubborn Starfish

Definition:
    Unreasonably obstinate, unyielding, resolute

Thoughts on Stubbornness:
    "Bow, stubborn knees!"
        (William Shakespeare)

"Facts are stubborn things; and whatever may be our wishes, our inclinations, or the dictates of our passions, they cannot alter the state of facts and evidence."
        (John Adams)

Excerpts from Classical Literature

"Then Obstinate laughed again. 'How many times am I to tell you that your Book is full of rubbish? There is not one word true. Now are you coming back or not?'

Obstinate looked very cross, and little Christian's heart began to beat faster and faster, but he answered bravely, 'No, I am going to the King . . .'

'No, thank you; I'm glad enough to get rid of you both.' And, with a mocking smile on his face, Obstinate turned back toward the City of Destruction."
    From: Little Pilgrim's Progress by Helen L. Taylor

"'Children,' he said, 'there is no worse sound in the world than somebody who cannot play the violin who insists on doing so anyway.'"
    From: Austere Academy: A Series of Unfortunate Events Book the Fifth by Lemony Snicket

NOUNS

his obduracy
authoritarian
a barrier
her determination
the gridlock
a hindrance
her inflexibility
an interference
the invincibleness
nonconformist
an obstacle
orneriness
a roadblock
stubbornness
stumbling block
unwillingness
her willfulness
his will of iron

NOUNS
Characters

a bull
a goat
a mule

52   Character Traits: Stubbornness

ADJECTIVES	ADVERBS	VERBS	ADDITIONAL WORDS
adamant	adamantly	argue	
balking	arbitrarily	bargain	
bullheaded	assertively	challenge	
cantankerous	authoritatively	clam up	
close-minded	categorically	counter	
difficult	convincingly	demand	
fixed	decidedly	disallow	
hardheaded	doggedly	disapprove	
inflexible	dogmatically	dissent	
mulish	emphatically	dodge	
obstinate	grimly	forbid	
persistent	inevitably	hold out	
pigheaded	intolerantly	ignore	
rebelling	relentlessly	lock	
relentless	solidly	object	
rigid	staunchly	obstruct	
single-minded	steadfastly	prevent	
strong-minded	stubbornly	protest	
tough	tenaciously	quibble	
unbending	tyrannically	refuse	
unbreakable	unalterably	repel	
uncooperative	unchangeably	scoff	
unmovable	unequivocally	stipulate	
unyielding	utterly	won't budge	

Words for Stubbornness

"Obstinacy is the result of the will forcing itself into the place of the intellect."
(Arthur Schopenhauer)

Words for Wisdom

A Wise Walrus

Definition:
    Being wise, having insight or discernment

Thoughts on Wisdom:
    "It wasn't raining when Noah built the ark."
                                  (Howard Ruff)

    "Live as if you were to die tomorrow.
     Learn as if you were to live forever."
                                  (Mahatma Gandhi)

Excerpts from Classical Literature

"His grandfather smiled. 'The best joy and beauty are the kinds that are unplanned, and the same is true of painting or poetry. Don't chew at it too much. It's beautiful, and it makes you remember a beautiful part of your life and that's enough.'"
                        From: Tracker by Gary Paulsen

"'This sister of mine, you must understand, is quite a different sort of person than myself . . . She is a very accomplished person, I assure you,' continued Quicksilver, 'and has all the arts and sciences at her fingers' ends. In short, she is so immoderately wise that many people call her wisdom personified.'"
        From: "The Gorgon's Head" by Nathaniel Hawthorne
      Excerpt from: Seventy Favorite Stories for Young Readers

NOUNS

his clarity
her depth
enlightenment
her foresight
horse sense
the judgment
his knowledge
her learning
her rationality
the reason
the sense
understanding
his wisdom
her wit

NOUNS
Characters

a professor
a sage
the scholar
a thinker

54   Character Traits: Wisdom

ADJECTIVES	ADVERBS	VERBS	ADDITIONAL WORDS
articulate	acutely	advise	
astute	assuredly	apprise	
aware	brilliantly	clarify	
brainy	cautiously	consult	
bright	clearly	contemplate	
comprehending	cleverly	counsel	
cultured	concisely	describe	
eagle-eyed	deeply	differentiate	
factual	distinctly	discern	
informed	exactly	edify	
insightful	exceptionally	educate	
intelligent	expertly	explain	
judicious	intelligently	guide	
keen	intentionally	illuminate	
knowing	judiciously	illustrate	
knowledgeable	noticeably	indicate	
perceptive	purposefully	indoctrinate	
piercing	raptly	judge	
prudent	rationally	lecture	
quick	subtly	observe	
reasonable	thoroughly	ponder	
sagacious	truthfully	teach	
scholarly	watchfully	uplift	
smart	wisely	wonder	

Words for Wisdom

"How much better to get wisdom than gold, to choose understanding rather than silver!"
Proverbs 16:16 NIV

My Title: _____

_____

Here is an open form for you to think of your own topic and related word lists. You may reproduce it and make as many copies as you need to express your own ideas.

Definition:

_____

Thoughts on _____

_____

_____

_____

Excerpts from Classical Literature

_____
_____
_____
_____
_____
_____
_____
_____

NOUNS

_____
_____
_____
_____
_____
_____
_____
_____
_____
_____
_____
_____
_____
_____
_____
_____
_____
_____
_____
_____

ADJECTIVES	ADVERBS	VERBS	ADDITIONAL WORDS
_____	_____	_____	_____
_____	_____	_____	_____
_____	_____	_____	_____
_____	_____	_____	_____
_____	_____	_____	_____
_____	_____	_____	_____
_____	_____	_____	_____
_____	_____	_____	_____
_____	_____	_____	_____
_____	_____	_____	_____
_____	_____	_____	_____
_____	_____	_____	_____
_____	_____	_____	_____
_____	_____	_____	_____
_____	_____	_____	_____
_____	_____	_____	_____
_____	_____	_____	_____
_____	_____	_____	_____
_____	_____	_____	_____
_____	_____	_____	_____

My Title: ☐

A Related Quotation:

Open Form for Student Originality

Section B

Words to Describe

Words to Describe Appearance 60

Words to Describe Color 62

Words to Describe Size 64

Words to Describe Time 66

Words to Describe Temperature 70

Words to Describe Texture 72

Words to Describe Shape 73

Words to Describe Appearance

ADJECTIVES to Describe Appearance

Seemingly Attractive	Seemingly Unattractive	Pleasant Attitudes	Unpleasant Attitudes
adorable	awful	cheerful	angry
beautiful	creepy	compassionate	bored
crystalline	dark	courageous	boring
cuddly	freaky	curious	complaining
cute	funny	determined	cowardly
distinctive	grotesque	ecstatic	crazy
elegant	homely	expert	critical
excellent	impossible	exuberant	dishonest
fabulous	outrageous	friendly	envious
fancy	ridiculous	generous	gossipy
fantastic	shadowy	happy	greedy
flashy	shady	honorable	hostile
glamorous	spooky	humorous	lawless
graceful	strange	humble	lethargic
perfect	terrible	imaginative	lonely
poised	ugly	meticulous	moody
quaint	uninviting	obedient	proud
sensational	unsightly	responsible	rude
terrific	unusual	solemn	selfish
wonderful	weird	wise	stubborn

60   Words to Describe: Appearance

ADJECTIVES for Choices of Style and Physical Appearance

bald	gorgeous
bearded	hairy
bedraggled	informal
casual	ornate
chic	picturesque
classical	plain
classy	plush
contemporary	popular
cosmopolitan	pretentious
country	regal
dashing	rich
dowdy	salty
dressy	scruffy
exquisite	simple
fashionable	sleazy
flamboyant	splendid
flowery	stately
folksy	stylish
formal	tacky
frumpy	trendy

VERBS for Changing Appearance

accessorize	embellish
adorn	enhance
arrange	groom
beautify	prepare
brush	primp
clad	refresh
cloth	straighten
comb	tidy
decorate	trim
dress	wear

ADDITIONAL WORDS

_____
_____
_____
_____
_____
_____
_____
_____

Words to Describe Appearance

"What a poor appearance the tales of poets make when stripped of the colors which music puts upon them, and recited in simple prose."

(Plato)

Words to Describe Color

ADVENTURES IN COLOR

The Colors live
Between black and white
In a land that we
Know best by sight.
But knowing best
Isn't everything,
For colors dance
And colors sing,
And colors laugh
And colors cry—
Turn off the light
And colors die,
And they make you feel
Every feeling there is
From the grumpiest grump
To the fizziest fizz.
And you and you and I
Know well
Each has a taste
And each has a smell
And each has a
  wonderful
Story to tell . . . .

From:
Hailstones and Halibut Bones:
Adventures in Color
by Mary O'Neill

ADJECTIVES to Describe Color

Brown
beige
chocolate
tan
umber

Black
charcoal
ebony
jet
licorice

Gray
battleship
mousy
silver
smoky

White
cream
ivory
oyster
pearl

Red
brick
burgundy
cardinal
cherry
crimson
pink
rose
ruby
scarlet

Purple
amethyst
fuchsia
lavender
lilac
mauve
mulberry
orchid
plum
violet

Blue
aqua
azure
cerulean
cobalt
marine
navy
royal
turquoise
violet

Green
apple
celery
grass
emerald
jade
lime
mint
moss
olive

Yellow
amber
apricot
blond
buttercup
canary
citron
gold
lemon
straw

Orange
carrot
mustard
ochre
peach
persimmon
pumpkin
salmon
tangerine
topaz

62   Words to Describe: Color

ADJECTIVES

Attributes of Color

Dull

ashen
colorless
drab
faded
pale

Neutral

clear
opaque
solid
translucent
transparent

Strong

bold
bright
colorful
gaudy
iridescent
vibrant
vivid

NOUNS

Values of Color

cast
complexion
dye
hue
luminosity
pigmentation
saturation
shade
tinge
value

Words for Light

beacon
beam
flash
flicker
glare
gleam
illumination
ray
reflection
spark

Familiar Sayings

Be careful you don't 'see red'.

"I'm feeling blue today!"

"She'll be green with envy."

"He has a colorful personality."

Words for light may be NOUNS or VERBS depending on how they are used in a sentence. Here is an example of each:

NOUN: "The gleam of the jewel awed us."
VERB: "The jewel gleamed brightly."

ADDITIONAL WORDS

Words to Describe Color

*"Like acrobats on a high trapeze the colors pose and bend their knees,
Twist and turn and leap and blend into shapes and feelings without end."*
From: Hailstones and Halibut Bones: Adventures in Color by Mary O'Neill

Words to Describe: Color 63

Words to Describe Size

ADJECTIVES to Describe Size

Large Amounts	Small or No Amounts	Large Sizes	Medium Sizes
abundant	any	astronomical	average
countless	empty	behemoth	medium
endless	few	colossal	middle-sized
enough	inadequate	enormous	moderate
full	insignificant	gargantuan	normal
gobs	insufficient	giant	standard
infinite	lacking	gigantic	
innumerable	little	great	**Small Sizes**
lavish	meager	Herculean	diminutive
legion	mere	huge	dwarfed
liberal	minimum	immense	itsy-bitsy
many	only	jumbo	little
multitudinous	scant	mammoth	microscopic
much	scarcely	massive	miniature
myriad	several	monstrous	minute
numerous	skimpy	monumental	petite
overflowing	some	sizable	puny
prolific	sparse	titanic	small
sufficient	stark	towering	tiny
well-stocked	unfilled	tremendous	wee

ADJECTIVES for Spaces and Measurements

Open Spaces

boundless
continued
extensive
immeasurable
limitless
open
roomy
spacious
vast

Tight Spaces

brimming
close
compact
crammed
cramped
crowded
jammed
loaded
stuffed

Length and Width Height and Depth

deep	alongside
distant	bordering
elongated	close
extended	flat
faraway	low
far	narrow
far-off	nearby
far-reaching	near
farther	nigh
further	pint-sized
high	shallow
lanky	short
lengthened	skinny
long	slender
remote	slight
stretching	slim
tall	spindly
telescopic	superficial
thick	tapered
wide	thin

ADDITIONAL WORDS

_____
_____
_____
_____
_____
_____

Words to Describe Size

"Truth is everlasting, but our ideas about truth are changeable. Only a little of the first fruits of wisdom, only a few fragments of the boundless heights, breadths and depths of truth, have I been able to gather."

(Martin Luther)

Words to Describe: Size 65

Words to Describe Time

ADJECTIVES

A Short Time
approaching
approximate
brief
close
coming
following
forthcoming
gone
imminent
impending
looming
nearing
quick

A Long Time
behind
belated
delayed
dragging
drawn-out
eternal
lasting
late
later
latter
lengthy
prolonged
unending

ADVERBS for Time Concepts

In the Past
ago
already
anciently
back
before
earlier
formerly
lately
once
previously
recently
since
yesterday

Present Time
currently
during
immediately
initially
instantly
momentarily
now
nowadays
presently
promptly
punctually
simultaneously
suddenly

In the Future
after
afterward
again
directly
eventually
finally
henceforth
later
next
soon
subsequently
tomorrow
ultimately

Adverbial Phrases
every now and then
hardly ever
off and on
on occasion
once in a blue moon
once in a while

ADDITIONAL WORDS
_____
_____
_____
_____
_____
_____

ADVERBIAL PHRASES for Time Concepts

Indefinite	In the Past	Now	In the Future
annually	a year ago	all of a sudden	after a while
intermittently	ages ago	at once	another time
infrequently	one time	at this moment	at a later date
irregularly	but once	at this time	at a later time
maybe	from way back	here and now	by and by
occasionally	in the olden days	in nothing flat	in a minute
perhaps	in times gone by	just now	in the aftermath
periodically	long ago	lickety-split	in the end
possibly	moments ago	on the double	in the future
sometimes	only once	on time	in the long run
sporadically	some time ago	right away	later on
yearly	time was	right now	one day
			once again
			once more
			one more time
			over again
			pretty soon
			sooner or later
			the next day

Most of the words on this page can easily work as <u>transitions</u> to help move the character or action from one event or place to the next. Use this page along with page ninety-four in the Appendix to keep your writing flowing along smoothly.

Excerpts from Classical Literature

"And now there was no mistaking it, and all four children stood blinking in the daylight of a winter day."

From: <u>The Lion, the Witch, and the Wardrobe</u> by C.S. Lewis

Words to Describe Time

"You may fool all the people some of the time, and some of the people all the time, but you cannot fool all the people all the time."

(Abraham Lincoln)

Words to Describe: Time 67

Words to Describe Time

NOUNS—PROPER and COMMON

Periods of Times

Months	Days	Measurement of Time	Specific Times of Day
January	Sunday	second	afternoon
February	Monday	minute	dawn
March	Tuesday	hour	dusk
April	Wednesday	day	evening
May	Thursday	week	midday
June	Friday	month	midnight
July	Saturday	year	morning
August	**Seasons**	decade	night
September	spring	century	noon
October	summer	millennium	sunrise
November	autumn	era	sunset
December	winter	eternity	twilight

Excerpts from Classical Literature

"Ramona continued to sit on the chair wiggling her tooth and being a very good girl as she had promised. The big hand crawled along to four. When it reached five, Ramona knew that it would be quarter after eight and time to go to school. A quarter was twenty-five cents. Therefore, a quarter past eight was twenty-five minutes after eight. She had figured the answer out all by herself."

From: <u>Ramona the Pest</u> by Beverly Cleary

ADDITIONAL WORDS

_____
_____
_____
_____
_____
_____

NOUNS

For Aging

- infant
- toddler
- child
- kid
- juvenile
- preteen
- teenager
- adolescent
- youth
- adult
- elder
- senior

ADJECTIVES for New and Old

For Maturity

- embryonic
- infantile
- babyish
- childish
- immature
- tender
- young
- full-grown
- mature
- aged
- old

For Older Things

- ancient
- antiquated
- antique
- archaic
- dated
- medieval
- old-fashioned
- original
- outdated
- quaint
- vintage

For Newer Things

- contemporary
- current
- futuristic
- innovative
- modern
- newfangled
- novel
- present-day
- recent
- ripe
- up-to-date

Phrases to Express the Need to Hurry (or Not)

"Be quick about it!"
"Don't dilly-dally!"
"Get a move on it!"
"Have patience!"

"Step on it!"
"Now's the time to do it!"
"Please be patient!"
"Wait a while!"

"Just a second"
"I can't wait!"
"I'm out of time!"
"Hurry up!"

Excerpts from Classical Literature

"Little Benjamin took one look, and then, in half a minute less than no time, he hid himself and Peter and the onions underneath a large basket."

From: The Tale of Benjamin Bunny by Beatrix Potter

Words to Describe Time

"Determine never to be idle. No person will have occasion to complain of the want of time who never loses any. It is wonderful how much may be done if we are always doing."

(Thomas Jefferson)

Words to Describe Temperature

NOUNS
For Hot Things
barbeque
desert
electricity
fever
fire
food
heat
heater
hotspring
jalapeno
lava
lightning
oven
radiator
stove
sun
temper
water
weather

ADJECTIVES
For Warmth
baking
blistering
boiling
broiling
burning
fiery
heated
hot
lukewarm
red-hot
roasting
scalding
scorching
sizzling
steamy
tepid
toasty
tropical
warm

Describing Weather
bitter
biting
blasting
bleak
brisk
crisp
cutting
drafty
intense
nippy
piercing
severe
shivery
snappy

VERBS
For Heating
bake
chafe
cook
heat
melt
toast

OUCH!

HOT!

OOH...O!

OW!

BURNING!

Excerpts from Classical Literature

"A large fire was built. Standing my dogs close to the warm heat, the gentle hands of the hunters went to work. With handkerchiefs and scarves heated steaming hot, little by little, the ice was thawed from their bodies."
From: Where the Red Fern Grows by Wilson Rawls

NOUNS	ADJECTIVES	VERBS	ADDITIONAL
For Cold Things	For Coldness	For Cooling	WORDS
air conditioner	bitter	air condition	
antarctic	chilly	defrost	
arctic	cold	freeze	
chilliness	cool	harden	
freezer	freezing	numb	
frost	frigid	refrigerate	
glacier	frosty		
hail	frozen	BRR.....R!	
ice	glacial	WHEW!	
ice cream	ice-capped		
icicle	iced	COLD!	
North Pole	icy		
refrigerator	numbing	CH..CH..!	
Popsicle	raw		
shivers	Siberian	CHILLY!	
snow	snow-capped		
weather	unheated	FREEZING!	

Excerpts from Classical Literature

"'Ah! Beautiful blue baby!' Paul said. He cradled the half-frozen calf in his great arms and carried it home. There he wrapped the baby ox in warm blankets and sat up all night taking care of it."

From: "Sky Bright Axe" by Adrien Stoutenburg

Words to Describe Temperature

"Forgiveness is an act of the will, and the will can function regardless of the temperature of the heart."
(Corrie ten Boom)

Words to Describe: Temperature 71

Words to Describe Texture

ADJECTIVES for Textures

Wetness
damp
drenched
gooey
moist
mushy
slimy
slushy
sticky
watery

Roughness
abrasive
bumpy
gritty
itchy
lumpy
sandy
prickly
sandpapery
tough

Fuzziness
cuddly
feathery
fibrous
furry
fuzzy
hairy
nappy
shaggy
soft

Cleanliness
clean
dirty
dusty
filthy
fresh
grimy
grubby
squeaky
washed

Dryness
arid
bone-dry
chapped
dehydrated
dried-out
parched
shriveled
thirsty

Smoothness
glossy
greasy
metallic
oily
satiny
silky
slick
tender

Tightness
rigid
stretched
taut
tightened

Hardness
concrete
firm
solid
unbending

Excerpts from Classical Literature

"'But supposing she turns the two leopards into stone?' whispered Lucy to Peter. I think the same idea had occurred to the leopards themselves; at any rate, as they walked off their fur was all standing up on their backs and their tails were bristling—like a cat's when it sees a strange dog."

From: The Lion, the Witch, and the Wardrobe by C.S. Lewis

Words to Describe Shape

ADJECTIVES

Triangular
acute
equilateral
isosceles
obtuse
scalene
triangular

Circular
ball-shaped
circular
circuitous
circling
round
winding

Rectangular
boxlike
oblong
parallelogram
quadratic
right-angled
square

ADDITIONAL
_____
_____
_____
_____
_____
_____
_____

For Lines
curved   contoured   proportional   straight
irregular   crooked   scalloped   winding

VERBS

Encircle
circulate
circumvent
encircle
enclose
encompass
loop
revolve

Square Off
align
balance
conform
level
make flush
match
straighten

NOUNS

Shapes
cone
hexagon
octagon
oval
rectangle
rhombus
trapezoid

Spheres
ball
earth
globe
marble
moon
orbit
planet

_____
_____
_____
_____
_____
_____
_____

Words to Describe Shape

"The earth takes shape like clay under a seal; its features stand out like those of a garment."
Job 38:14

Section C

Words for Movement and the Senses

Words for Feet 76

Words for Hands 78

Words for Hearing 80

Words for Seeing 82

Words for Smelling 84

Words for Speaking 86

Words for Thinking 88

Words for Feet

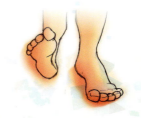

NOUNS Related to Feet

Things to Put on Feet
booties
boots
cast
flippers
footwear
galoshes
ice skates
leggings
mukluks
roller skates
shoes
slippers
snowshoes
socks
work boots

Words for Human Feet
barefoot
big toe
feet
foot
pinky
toe

Words for Animal Feet
claw
feet
forefoot
hoof
hooves
paw

Places for Feet to Move
dance floor
dirt
field
floor
ground
hill
house
ice
land
mountain
path
river
snow
stump
water

ADVERBS

How Feet Might Move
awkwardly
calmly
energetically
gently
gracefully
halfheartedly
hurriedly
impulsively
lazily
powerfully
quietly
slightly
sprightly
weakly
wildly

Excerpts from Classical Literature

"To solve the muddle, Paul built a colossal flapjack griddle. The surface was greased by kitchen helpers with slabs of bacon laced to their feet."

From: Paul Bunyan by Steven Kellogg

76   Words for Movement: Feet

VERBS for Moving Feet

ADDITIONAL WORDS

Faster Movements
bolt
bound
charge
dash
dart
gallop
lurch
scamper
scramble
skip
spring

Slower Movements
amble
crawl
creep
edge
meander
plod
saunter
shuffle
slink
totter
trudge

Other Foot Actions
crouch
hike
jump
kick
kneel
lumber
lunge
pace
pounce
pound
prance
rumble
scoot
splash
slosh
thump
thunder
tramp
walk
wander

Graceful Movements
coast
float
glide
sail
skate
skim
sway

Awkward Movements
flail
hobble
limp
skid
stub
stumble
trip

Words for Feet

"Think of the magic of that foot, comparatively small, upon which your whole weight rests. It's a miracle, and the dance . . . is a celebration of that miracle."
(Martha Washington)

Words for Movement: Feet

Words for Hands

NOUNS about Hands

Things to Put on Hands
bandage
brace
bracelet
cast
glove
lotion
mitt
mitten
muff
nail polish
ring
soap
string

Words for Human Hands
finger
fingernail
fist
hand
knuckle
palm
wrist

Related to Animals' Paws
claw
paw
pincher

PREPOSITIONAL PHRASES

Hand Positions
above the shoulders
at his fingertips
behind the back
beyond their reach
in the air
into her hand
near his arm
out of her hand
over the head
through her fingers
toward it
under her hand
against his arm

ADVERBS

How Hands Might Move
carefully
evenly
gingerly
firmly
forcefully
loosely
roughly
securely
steadily
suddenly
swiftly
tenderly
tightly

Excerpts from Classical Literature

"[Paddington] jumped up, meaning to raise his hat, and in his haste slipped on a patch of strawberry jam which somehow or other had found its way on to the glass table-top. For a brief moment he had a dizzy impression of everything and everyone being upside down. He waved his paws wildly in the air and then, before anyone could catch him, he somersaulted backwards and landed with a splash in his saucer of tea."

From: The Adventures of Paddington by Michael Bond

VERBS for Moving Hands

Pleasant Movements
cradle
cuddle
enfold
feel
handle
massage
pet
signal
tickle
touch
wave
wiggle

Unpleasant Movements
flap
jerk
pinch
point
poke
push
scratch
tremble

Other Hand Actions
catch
clap
draw
fasten
finger
gather
hammer
paint
pass
pick
reach
rub
signal
sign
stroke
tap
throw
touch
twirl
twist
wrap
write

Holding on Movements
clasp
clinch
cling
clutch
grab
grasp
grip
pluck
pull
snatch
squeeze
tug

ADDITIONAL WORDS

_____
_____
_____
_____
_____
_____
_____
_____
_____
_____
_____
_____

Excerpts from Classical Literature

"Before her stroke, Grandma had appliquéd all of the design, adding a border of deep blue cloth, and started the quilting. In the past, Grandma's quick, sure fingers would have flown through the rest. Now it was up to Ariel . . . . The quilting seemed agonizingly slow. Ariel made a lot of mistakes. She had to pull out stitches, and she pricked her fingers. Worst of all was sitting inside when the weather outside was so inviting."
From: The Canada Geese Quilt by Natalie Kinsey-Warnock

Words for Hands

"Let us raise a standard to which the wise and honest can repair; the rest is in the hands of God."
(George Washington)

Words for Hearing

NOUNS or VERBS

Animal Sounds	Object Sounds	Human Sounds
bark	clatter	cry
bleat	clank	groan
bray	crackle	growl
buzz	crash	laugh
coo	hum	moan
hiss	jangle	murmur
meow	jingle	patter
moo	knock	outcry
neigh	pop	rasp
peep	racket	scream
purr	rattle	speech
roar	rustle	twitter
screech	smash	wail
squawk	whirr	whisper
squeak	whoosh	whistle
squeal		
snarl		
snort		
whine		
whinny		

ADJECTIVES

For Loud Sounds	For Quiet Sounds
alarming	calming
blaring	hushed
blasting	inaudible
cacophonous	lulling
deafening	mellow
discordant	melodious
grating	muffled
jarring	mute
loud	quiet
noisy	relaxing
penetrating	peaceful
piercing	serene
ringing	silent
shrill	still
thunderous	soothing

Human, animal, and object noises may be nouns or verbs depending on how they are used in a sentence. For example:

NOUN: *"The bark of the dog was heard far away."*
VERB: *"The dog barked so loudly it woke me up."*

80   Words for the Senses: Hearing

NOUNS	VERBS for Hearing		ADDITIONAL WORDS
Things that Make Sounds	**Listening**	**Verb Phrases**	
audience	attend	become aware	_____
band	auscultate	become informed	_____
choir	catch	close his ears	_____
harmony	eavesdrop	cover his ears	_____
machine	hear	is all ears	_____
melody	hearken	learn of	_____
music	hear out	listen in	_____
orchestra	heed	pay attention	_____
radio	listen	prick up her ears	_____
speech	overhear	shut out	_____
symphony	pick up	tune in	_____
voice	receive	tune out	_____
	wiretap	turn a deaf ear	_____

Excerpts from Classical Literature

"Stamp! Stamp! Stamp! Slap! Slap! That's all he could remember of it. A great deal of stamping and slapping. His boots made a terrific clatter and his trousers kept up that whistling and squeaking. He had never felt more foolish and miserable in his whole life. He could hardly hear the music. Miss Chichester kept time by clapping her hands very hard and nodding her head back and forth so that the hairpins flew."

From: "The Moffats and the Sailor's Hornpipe" by Eleanor Estes

Words for Hearing

"Trouble knocked on the door, but, hearing laughter, hurried away."
(Benjamin Franklin)

Words for the Senses: Hearing

Words for Seeing

NOUNS
Words Related to Seeing

brilliance	picture
depiction	reflection
eye	rubberneck
floodlight	scout
glint	sentinel
highlight	spectacle
illusion	splendor
illustration	spotlight
image	spotter
light	spy
lookout	surveillance
mirage	twinkle
panorama	view

ADJECTIVES
Use of the Eyes

alert
frowning
imaginative
watchful

Adjective Phrases

bright eyed
evil eyed
glassy eyed
hawk eyed
open eyed
starry eyed
wide eyed

How Things Appear

blinding
bright
brilliant
dazzling
flaming
flashy
fleeting
flickering
gleaming
glistening
glowing
gorgeous
illuminating
lifeless
obvious
showy
sparkling
ugly
vacant
visible

Excerpts from Classical Literature

"But Tito saw none of these things. He was blind—had been blind from birth.... But that did not make him sorry for himself. If he could not see the sights that delighted the lads of Pompeii, he could hear and smell things they never noticed. He could really see more with his ears and nose than they could with their eyes. When he and Bimbo went out walking, he knew just where they were going and exactly what was happening."

From: "The Dog of Pompeii" by Louis Untermeyer

ADVERBS	VERBS for Seeing		ADDITIONAL WORDS
menacingly	blink	scan	
piercingly	blur	scowl	
visually	envision	sight	
warily	eye	skim	
witheringly	gawk	spy	
VARIOUS PHRASES	gaze	spot	
catch sight of	glance	squint	
glaze over	glare	stare	
in plain sight	glimpse	survey	
look-alike	look	view	
ray of light	notice	visualize	
under one's nose	peek	watch	
	peer	wink	

Excerpts from Classical Literature

"Each day the sun peeped in at the south windows. It made everything look bright and beautiful. The grandmother lived on the north side of the house. The sun never came to her room . . . . Elsa tried and tried to think how she could carry the sunshine to her grandmother . . . . 'I know, I'll take them [the sun rays] in my dress. Look, Grandma, look! I have some sunshine for you . . .' but there was not a ray to be seen.

'It peeps out of your eyes, my child,' said her grandmother, 'and it shines in your sunny, golden hair. I do not need the sun when I have you with me.'"

From: "Little Sunshine" Retold by Etta Austin Blaisdell & Mary Frances Blaisdell

Words for Seeing

"Some men see things as they are and say, 'Why?' I dream of things that never were, and say, 'Why not?'"
(George Bernard Shaw)

Words for Smelling

NOUNS Related to Smelling

Pleasant Smells
aroma
bouquet
cologne
fragrance
nectar
perfume
sachet
scent
smell
spice
trace
whiff

Unpleasant Smells
foulness
fume
odor
smoke
stench

For Odd Smells
bark
gasoline
oil
grease
turpentine

Smelly Places
bakery
barn
dump
field
fishery
garden
gym
hospital
kitchen
restaurant
stable
track

ADJECTIVES

Pleasant Smells
appetizing
aromatic
clean
gingery
heavenly
inviting
luscious
piney
savory
spicy
sweet
tempting

Unpleasant Smells
acrid
awful
burnt
damp
earthy
fishy
foul
loathsome
moldy
musty
pungent
putrid
rancid
rank
revolting
sickening
strong
yucky

Excerpts from Classical Literature

"The smell that came from under the lid wasn't possum. It was ham bone. The boy had only smelled it twice in his life, once before in his own cabin, and once when he was walking past the big house down the road. The sausage and ham bone smells filled up the cabin and leaked out through the cracks in the floor and around the door. They excited Sounder, and now he was scratching at the door."

From: Sounder by William H. Armstrong

ADVERBS

How Things Might Smell Good
attractively
deliciously
freshly
impressively
lightly
pleasantly
undeniably

How Things Might Smell Bad
detestably
heavily
horribly
obnoxiously
oddly
offensively
revoltingly

VERBS

Related to Smelling
deodorize
detect
drift
emit
engulf
fill
freshen
inhale
permeate
reek
smell
sniff
stink
waft

ADDITIONAL WORDS

_____
_____
_____
_____
_____
_____
_____
_____
_____
_____
_____
_____
_____
_____

NOUNS for Spices

allspice	garlic	oregano
basil	ginger	rosemary
apple cider	nutmeg	sage
cinnamon	onion	thyme

Excerpts from Classical Literature

"My eyes widened and tears came. Then the door opened and wind blew in with Papa, and I went to stir the stew. Papa put his arms around me and put his nose in my hair.

'Nice soapy smell, that stew,' he said.

I laughed. 'That's my hair.'"

From: Sarah, Plain and Tall by Patricia MacLachlan

Words for Smelling

"Forgiveness is the fragrance that the violet sheds on the heel that has crushed it."
(Mark Twain)

Words for Speaking

General Terms

NOUNS
Ways to Speak
accent
dialect
drawl
jargon
lingo
slang
translation
utterance
ventriloquism
verbalization
vocalization

HI!

THANKS!

MAY I?

COOL!

GOOD!

VERBS
Ways to Speak
babble
chant
chatter
cry
drone
gab
grumble
heckle
intone
laugh
patter
prattle
rap
rhapsodize
sing
spout
squeal
stammer
vocalize
whine
yak

Positive or Neutral Speech

ADJECTIVES
candid
complimentary
diverse
electrifying
eloquent
emphatic
expressive
fluent
humorous
informative
impassioned
impressive
insistent
meaningful
metaphorical
moving
profound
significant
symbolic
touching
unique
unusual
well-expressed

VERBS
Positive
advise
agree
affirm
appreciate
apologize
assert
commend
compliment
confide
consult
defend
elaborate
exclaim
pardon
praise
pray
proclaim
promise
propose
thank
urge
vindicate

VERBS
Neutral
answer
appeal
ask
clarify
comment
contact
contradict
converse
describe
exchange
explain
express
hint
influence
inform
instruct
label
network
persuade
question
read
warn

86 Words for the Senses: Speaking

General Terms

NOUNS

argument
commentary
conference
consultation
conversation
dialogue
dissertation
interview
explanation
instruction
introduction
lecture
meeting
monologue
narration
negotiation
oration
paraphrase
recitation
seminar
sermon
symposium

Negative Speech

ADJECTIVES

abusive
ambiguous
critical
cynical
degrading
evasive
forceful
foreboding
glib
hateful
illogical
long-winded
misleading
obnoxious
opinionated
outspoken
provocative
sarcastic
scornful
stilted
thundering
vague

VERBS

allege
argue
confide
criticize
decree
demand
deny
divulge
fabricate
insinuate
insist
jabber
mock
pester
plead
protest
quarrel
ridicule
scoff
slander
squabble
taunt

ADDITIONAL WORDS

Words for Speaking

"Pleasant words are a honeycomb, sweet to the soul and healing to the bones."
Proverbs 16:24 NIV

Words for Thinking

NOUNS

Thoughts and the Mind

belief	hope
brain	idea
brainstorm	impression
brainwork	intention
concept	intuition
conclusion	mastermind
conjecture	mind
design	notion
dream	opinion
egghead	prodigy
guess	theory
highbrow	thought

ADJECTIVES

Thoughts and the Mind

absorbing	inept
anxious	innocent
canny	intellectual
captivating	logical
confusing	loony
deliberate	meaningless
diplomatic	meditative
discreet	mindless
engrossed	musing
exciting	natural
farsighted	philosophical
harebrained	provocative
	preoccupied
	rapt
	rational
	refreshing
	riveting
	suspicious
	sympathetic

Excerpts from Classical Literature

"Mark stood beside him, a hand on the broad head, absently rubbing the base of the tulip-shaped ears, and thinking. At any minute the man who had won the right to kill Ben might come up the trail. He thought of his dream. It had been so real. That's just how it will be, he thought . . . . Then another thought entered his mind . . . . The thought was so shocking that at first his mind refused to accept it. But the more he thought about it, the more logical it became."

From: <u>Gentle Ben</u> by Walt Morey

88   Words for the Senses: Thinking

ADVERBS

How People Might Think

inadvertently
curiously
inwardly
knowingly
meaningfully
mindfully
understandably
wisely

VARIOUS PHRASES

chew on it
empty-headed
figure it out
had a hunch
hazard a guess
know-how
lamebrained
lost in thought
mull it over
stew over it

VERBS

Acting on Thoughts

analyze	know
brainwash	meditate
convince	perceive
create	persuade
educate	plan
hypothesize	realize
indoctrinate	reason
influence	reflect
instill	speculate
intuit	think
invent	weigh

ADDITIONAL WORDS

_____
_____
_____
_____
_____
_____
_____
_____
_____
_____
_____

Excerpts from Classical Literature

"The flight ended only just in time for him, just before his arm gave way. He loosed Dori's ankles with a gasp and fell onto the rough platform of an eagle's eyrie. There he lay without speaking and his thoughts were a mixture of surprise at being saved from the fire, and fear lest he fell off that narrow place into the deep shadows on either side."

From: The Hobbit by J.R.R. Tolkien

Words for Thinking

"Watch your thoughts, for they become words. Watch your words, for they become actions. Watch your actions, for they become habits. Watch your habits, for they become character. Watch your character, for it becomes your destiny."

(Unknown)

Words for the Senses: Thinking

Section D
Appendix

Playing with Words - Make It Fun! 92

Transition Words Not Related to Time 94

Prepositions - Excellent for Memorization 95

Categories of Literary Genres 96

Definitions and Examples of Literary Devices 98

Playing with Words - Make It Fun!

"A word fitly spoken is like apples of gold in pictures of silver." Proverbs 25:11

A Word *Write* Now Teaching Tips

Playing with Words is fun for everyone.

If you are enthusiastic and playful with words, your students will be too. Sections B and C lend themselves well to begin work with word play. Start simply by introducing *Words to Describe Color*. Pick a common object, such as the sun. Read the lists of color words for yellow, orange, and red, discussing the various colors the sun might be in different situations. Together, verbally create sentences about the sun, using color words. You might say, "At noon the sun is bright yellow, but when it sets it takes on a deep, golden glow."

Introduce one page at a time, adding new concepts to your previous sentences and creating entirely new ones. For example, you might go next to *Words to Describe Size*. Here the words are categorized by large and small amounts, large and small sizes, open and tight spaces, as well as length, width, height and depth. Find many different words to describe the sun. You might say: "At noon, the bright yellow sun seems far away, but when it sets with its deep, golden glow, it appears immense in the western sky." Keep a list for future reference. There are no limits to the possibilities or variety of responses.

Section A: Character Traits

Section A is great to simply read and discuss any given trait. It offers endless hours of playful discussion, since everyone will have experienced many of the various emotions portrayed sooner or later. It's fun to invent a character and verbally play with words and sentences to develop interesting problems and settings that fit his or her basic nature. Keep notes and allow such play to develop into unique story characters naturally. Using the quotations in Section A provides a built-in opportunity to step into the author's shoes to discover how his character conveys that trait through his words, his actions, his thoughts, or through another's eyes.

Another idea would be to reflect on the characters in a story currently being enjoyed. Using the Section A, *Table of Contents*, assign the dominant two traits each character is exhibiting. Look up the lists for those traits and refine the trait by selecting the most accurate and precise terms for his or her behavior from the lists. Now use those in a sentence or two to show knowledge of the story characters.

More Teaching Tips—Using Titles to Find Words

Learning to categorize and classify information is a critical learning skill that will apply to all curriculum areas. It is often overlooked in the day-to-day academic challenges but is a foundational and valuable skill. Sections B and C are great places to develop the ability to quickly and efficiently connect the labels to the words in the list.

The Category Game will help build awareness of the organizational structure of *A Word Write Now*. Together, leaf through the book, discovering interesting themes, words, and groupings. Read the *Table of Contents* aloud, commenting on anything of interest as you go. Work on one section at a time, beginning with Section B or C.

To play, one person secretly opens to any page in a designated section, chooses a word, and reads it aloud. The other participants must quickly decide under which category that word might be listed, using the *Table of Contents* for that section as a reference. For example, a student might read the word *now*. Players need to decide that *now* is located under *Time*. The quickest one finds the next word and so on.

The more familiar the contents are to the student, the more readily he or she will be able to locate an appropriate list of words when his or her mind is focused on writing and choosing the right word. Warming up every day with such play will benefit the student throughout the day's curriculum challenges. With over 1600 different words in Section A - Character Traits, plus well over 1000 more in Sections B and C, there are endless possibilities for vocabulary development. To further extend the activity, any given word can also take the young explorer straight to a good thesaurus for more investigation. Every effort has been made to avoid duplicating words. Occasionally, a word will be used under a different category, but that is rare and purposeful.

The Sub-Category Game will help build awareness of the specific contents under each category in Sections A, B, and C. Play the same as above, but limit the word choice to one column, such as *Words for Hearing*. With the book open, the participants must quickly identify the subcategory. For example: under *Words for Hearing*, the word *jangle* is listed under the subtitle, *Object Sound*. Early readers can enjoy playing as well when the words choices are read aloud to them.

While these are simple activities, not focused on winning or losing, any kind of activity to build familiarity and ease in using A Word Write Now will benefit the student when his or her mind is on quickly locating the perfect word so the writing task may continue, which of course, is the goal.

Transition Words Not Related to Time

To Indicate More Information

Additionally
Also
Besides
Furthermore
Indeed
Moreover
Second, Third, etc.

To Summarize

Briefly
In brief
Overall
Summarizing
Summing up
To put it briefly
To sum up
To summarize

To Indicate an Example

For example
For instance
In particular
Particularly
Specifically
To demonstrate
To illustrate

To Conclude

Given these facts
Hence
In conclusion
So
Therefore
Thus
To conclude
Finally

To Compare or Contrast

Although
Conversely
However
In comparison
In contrast
Likewise
Nevertheless
On the other hand
Similarly
Whereas
Yet

To Indicate Importance

Absolutely
Distinctly
Essentially
Fundamentally
Notably
Primarily
Relatively
Seriously
Significantly
Substantially

To Show Assurance

Assuredly
Definitely
Evidently
Normally
Obviously
Predictably
Probably
Strictly
Typically
Undeniably

Prepositions - Excellent for Memorization

about	before	in front of	regarding
above	behind	in regard to	since
according to	beneath	inside	through
across	beside	in spite of	throughout
after	between	instead	to
against	beyond	instead of	toward
ahead of	by	into	under
along	concerning	like	underneath
along with	despite	minus	unlike
amid	down	near	until
among	due to	of	up
around	during	off	upon
as	except	on	up to
as for	except for	on account of	with
as to	for	onto	within
aside from	from	opposite	without
at	in	out	
atop	in addition to	outside	
away from	in back of	over	
because of	in case of	past	

Cat in the Cactus!

Excerpts from Classical Literature

"Then the shape, tossed and bent under the wind, lifted the latch of the gate, and they could see that it belonged to a woman, who was holding her hat on with one hand and carrying a bag in the other. As they watched, Jane and Michael saw a curious thing happen. As soon as the shape was inside the gate the wind seemed to catch her up into the air and fling her at the house. It was as though it had flung her first at the gate, waited for her to open it, and then had lifted and thrown her, bag and all, at the front door. The watching children heard a terrific bang, and as she landed the whole house shook . . . This is your new nurse, Mary Poppins. Jane and Michael, say how do you do!'"

From: *Mary Poppins* by P.L. Travers

Appendix: Prepositions - Excellent for Memorization

Categories of Literary Genres

Definitions:

Genre: a kind or type of work of literature or art which is distinguished by subject, theme, or style

Fiction: all written work which is made up of imaginary characters, events, or places . . . It may be *true-to-life*, but isn't true.

Nonfiction: all written work which is based completely on known, true facts

Prose: the ordinary form of written or spoken language, without rhyme or meter; not poetry

Thoughts on knowing about genres:

"The analysis of different types of literature promotes cognitive development because it gives students an opportunity to apply similar skills and strategies, such as identifying themes discussed in one genre—fiction, for example—to other genres like poetry, reports, descriptive pieces, and plays.

(Carl B. Smith)

NONFICTION	NONFICTION	NONFICTION
almanac	expository	philosophy
article	famous places	photographic
atlas	history	political
autobiography	how-to book	reference
biography	journal	science
commentary	letters	speech
diary	literary criticism	spiritual
dictionary	magazine	statute
documentary	manual	technical
encyclopedia	memoir	textbook
essay	narrative nonfiction	travelogue

GENRES

Fiction
adventure
allegory
anecdote
comedy
comic books
epic
fable
fairy tale
fantasy
folk tale
Gothic novel
historical fiction
horror
humor
legend
mystery
myth
novel
novella
picaresque
quest
realistic fiction
romance
science fiction
short story
suspense
tall tale

Drama
chronicle play
comedy
epilogue
farce
fantasy
masque
medieval mystery
melodrama
monologue
musical
problem play
satire
soliloquy
tragedy

Poetry
abc poem
acrostic
ballad
ballade
blank verse
burlesque
cinquain
couplet
dramatic monologue
elegy
epic
epigram
epitaph
free verse
haiku
Horatian ode
iambic pentameter
idyll
limerick
lyric
ode
pastoral
petrarchan
romanticism
rhymed verse
quatrain
sonnet

Appendix: Genres 97

Definitions and Examples of Literary Devices

"Let your speech be always with grace, seasoned with salt, that ye may know how ye ought to answer every man."
Colossians 4:6 KJV

Alliteration

Definition: Repeating the same beginning consonant or blended sounds in two or more words or phrases.

Example: The wise walrus wondered why wisdom waned in the world.

Allusion

Definition: An indirect reference or a casual mention in a literary work to a person, place, a thing or an event that is already well known.

Example: The judge sent the lawless lobster to "the big house."

Ambiguity

Definition: Using language which conveys two or more possible meanings simultaneously; expressions which are vague or not clear in meaning.

Example: Wrapping his tail around the seaweed, the dizzy, honorable sea horse mentioned to the dishonest devil ray that he needed to keep himself "on the level" for a while.

Assonance

Definition: Vowel rhyme, or words that have the same vowel sound, in which the consonant sounds are not the same.

Example: The proud puffer fish loudly shouted his accomplishments to the crowd.

Cacophony

Definition: Noise, or harsh, jarring sounds; an unpleasant combinations of sounds; dissonance.

Example: Enraged, the angry orca yowled, snarled and thundered uncontrollably.

98 Appendix: Definitions and Examples of Literary Devices

Caricature

Definition: "Use of exaggeration or distortion (physical characteristic, eccentricity, personality trait, or exaggerated act) to make a figure appear comic or ridiculous." (Hall)

Example: While her whiskers tickled in the unfamiliar clumps of seaweed, the curious catfish poked her nose here and there, mumbling, "Just looking."

Consonance

Definition: Repeating consonant sounds in the middle or at the end of words (brought, comfort).

Example: The compassionate dolphin heartily brought comfort to all she met.

Hyperbole

Definition: Using deliberate and obvious exaggeration as a figure of speech; not meant to be taken literally.

Example: The bright smile of the cheerful clownfish blinded the hostile shark, calming him immediately.

Idiom

Definition: A commonly heard phrase or expression that has a meaning that differs from the literal meaning, such as *It's raining cats and dogs*.

Example: Quaking in his boots, the fearful flounder fled.

Irony

Definition: "Contrast between expected outcomes or what appears to be and the actual way things turn out; useful to humorously comment upon the unpredictable nature of life. Three main literary forms of irony: verbal, situation, dramatic." (Hall)

Example: When gripped by the green-eyed monster, the envious eel impulsively left the safety of her rocky crevice, only to be coveted as a snack by an even larger gluttonous foe.

Appendix: Definitions and Examples of Literary Devices

Metaphor

Definition: A figure of speech that doesn't use the words *like* or *as,* but does suggest a similarity between two different concepts, such as "the storm raged."

Example: The sea otter became a beach ball, exuberantly bouncing through the waves.

Meter and Rhyme

Definition: Meter is the rhythm made by the arrangement of stressed and unstressed syllables in poetry. Rhyme is the repetition of similar or identical sounds at the end of words.

Example: The stubborn starfish would not budge;
he said he would not share his fudge.

Onomatopoeia

Definition: Words that are made up to imitate the actual sound of the object or action involved, such as *bang* or *wham*.

Example: "Sheesh. Tsk, tsk," muttered the critical carp with disgust.

Personification

Definition: "A figure of speech that assigns human qualities, actions, characteristics, or personality to an animal, an object, a natural force, or an idea." (Hall)

Example: The generous manatee magnanimously offered praise to the blushing humble oyster.

Repetition

Definition: Repeating words, phrases, "-ing" or "-ly" words, adjectives, nouns, or verbs are examples of stylistic techniques in sentences. (Pudewa)

Example: Deceiving his partners, daring his opponents, and developing his plans were everyday activities for the dishonest devil ray.

Simile:

Definition: Using the words *like, as, such as,* or *than* to compare two unlike things which have some clear similarity to each other.

Example: The gossipy octopus leaked secrets like a sieve.

Stereotype:

Definition: "Fixed generalized ideas about characters and situations such as plots, predictable formula or recognizable pattern; persons typed rather than unique, denied full range of qualities and characteristics." (Hall)

Example: The shiftless lionfish spent his time lazily lying around the house.

Understatement:

Definition: Not showing the true significance of something; understating its importance with words or actions.

Example: After the courageous penguin's dramatic rescue of the complaining carp, the hero quietly replied, "No big deal."

Very Short Sentence:

Definition: A sentence of five or less words, often used for dramatic effect. Three short staccato sentences create an even more dramatic language pattern. (Pudewa)

Example: "Must get to shore. Must get to shore." The responsible sea turtle crooned her quiet tune rhythmically as she trudged through the sand.

There are many more literary devices of great value for you to discover on your own. Here are twenty more for you to check out.

1. Analogy
2. Aphorism
3. Atmosphere
4. Cliché
5. Figure of Speech
6. Flashback
7. Flash-forward
8. Foreshadowing
9. Imagery
10. Inference
11. Paradox
12. Parallel Story
13. Parody
14. Poetic Justice
15. Pun
16. Rhythm
17. Satire
18. Symbolism
19. Theme
20. Tone

Bibliography

Adams, John. Quoted from ThinkExist. http://www.thinkexist.com (accessed April 12, 2010).

Alcott, Louisa May. "Christmas at the Marches." *The Bookshelf for Boys and Girls*. New York: The University Society, Inc., 1965.

Andersen, Hans Christian. "The Nightingale." *Elements of Literature Introductory Course*. Austin: Holt, Rinehart and Winston, 1993.

Andersen, Hans Christian. "The Emperor's New Clothes." *Elements of Literature Introductory Course*. Austin: Holt, Rinehart and Winston, 1993.

Andrews, Adam and Missy. *Teaching the Classics: A Socratic Method for Literary Education*. Washington: The Center for Literary Education, 2004.

Aristotle. Quoted from ThinkExist. http://www.thinkexist.com (accessed April 12, 2010).

Armstrong, William H. *Sounder*. New York: HarperCollins Publishers, 1969.

Austen, Jane. *Pride and Prejudice*. New York: Playmore Inc. Publishers and Waldman Publishing Corp., 1997.

Baldwin, James. "The King and His Hawk." *The Children's Book of Virtues*. New York: Simon & Schuster, Inc., 1995.

Banks, Lynne Reid. *The Indian in the Cupboard*. New York: Doubleday and Company, Inc., 1980.

Blaisdell, Etta and Mary Frances Blaisdell. "Little Hero of Holland." *The Children's Book of Virtues*. New York: Simon & Schuster, Inc., 1995.

Blaisdell, Etta and Mary Frances Blaisdell. "Little Sunshine." *The Children's Book of Virtues*. New York: Simon & Schuster, Inc., 1995.

Bond, Michael. *The Adventures of Paddington*. Great Britain: Hartnolls Ltd., 1990.

Brussell, Eugene E., ed. *Webster's New World Dictionary of Quotable Definitions*. New Jersey, Prentice Hall, 1988.

Burnett, Frances Hodgson. *The Secret Garden*. New York: Sterling Publishing Co., Inc. 2004.

Byron, Lord. Quoted from ThinkExist. http://www.thinkexist.com (accessed April 12, 2010).

Chaucer, Geoffrey. Quoted from ThinkExist. http://www.thinkexist.com (accessed April 12, 2010).

Chesterton, G.K. *The Ballad of the White Horse*. Project Gutenberg. http://www.gutenberg.org/ (accessed April 28, 2010).

Clark, Frank A. Quoted from ThinkExist. http://www.thinkexist.com (accessed April 12, 2010).

Cleary, Beverly. *Henry and Ribsy*. New York: William Morrow and Company, Inc., 1954.

Cleary, Beverly. *The Mouse and the Motorcycle*. New York: William Morrow and Company, Inc., 1965.

Cleary, Beverly. *Ramona the Pest*. New York: William Morrow and Company, Inc., 1968.

Dickens, Charles. "A Christmas Carol." *The Bookshelf for Boys and Girls*. New York: The University Society, Inc., 1965.

Dobbs, Rose. *Grimm's Fairy Tales*. New York: Random House, Inc., 1955.

Edelstein, Linda N. *Writer's Guide to Character Traits, 2nd Edition*. Cincinnati, OH: Writer's Digest Books, 2006.

Ehrmann, Max. *Desiderata*. Kansas City, MO: Andrews McMeel Publishing, LLC, 1927.

Erwin, Paul R. *The Winston Grammar Program*. Battle Ground, WA: Precious Memories Educational Resources, 1995.

Estes, Eleanor. "The Hundred Dresses." *70 Favorite Stories for Young Readers*. New York: Reader's Digest Association, Inc., 1974.

Estes, Eleanor. "The Moffats and the Sailor's Hornpipe." *70 Favorite Stories for Young Readers*. New York: Reader's Digest Association, Inc., 1974.

Frank, Anne. Quoted from BrainyQuote. http://www.thinkexist.com (accessed April 12, 2010).

Franklin, Benjamin. Quoted from ThinkExist. http://www.thinkexist.com (accessed April 12, 2010).

Frost, Robert. Quoted from ThinkExist. http://www.thinkexist.com. (accessed April 12, 2010).

Gandhi, Mahatma. Quoted from ThinkExist. http://www.thinkexist.com (accessed April 12, 2010).

Gauch, Patricia Lee. *Christina Katerina & the Box*. New York: Penguin Group, 1971.

George, Jean Craighead. *My Side of the Mountain*. New York: Puffin Books, 1991.

Gillepsie, Joseph. *Herndon's Informants*. Edited by Douglas L. Wilson and Rodney D. Davis. Champaign, IL: University of Illinois Press, 1997.

Hall, Susan. *Using Picture Storybooks to Teach Literary Devices*. Westport, CT: Oryx Press, 1990.

Hawthorne, Nathaniel. "The Gorgon's Head." *70 Favorite Stories for Young Readers*. New York: Reader's Digest Association, Inc., 1976.

Henry, Marguerite. *King of the Wind*. New York: Aladdin Paperbacks, 1948.

Herriot, James. *James Herriot's Treasury for Children*. New York: St. Martin's Press, 1986.

Hurwitz, Isacher. Quoted from HealthGroup. http://health.group.yahoo.com (accessed April 28, 2010).

Jefferson, Thomas. Quoted from BrainyQuote. http://www.brainyquote.com (accessed April 12, 2010).

Johnson, Samuel. Quoted from Thinkexist.com. http://www.thinkexist.com (accessed April 12, 2010).

Josephson, Michael. "That's Just the Way I Am." CharacterCounts! http://www.charactercounts.org (accessed April 12, 2010).

Keller, Helen. Quoted from BrainyQuote. http://www.brainyquote.com (accessed April 12, 2010).

Kellogg, Steven. *Paul Bunyan*. Columbus, OH: Atlas Editions, Inc., 1984.

Kinsey-Warnock, Natalie. *The Canada Geese Quilt*. New York: Puffin Books, 1989.

Lewis, C.S. *The Chronicles of Narnia: The Lion, the Witch, and the Wardrobe*. New York: HarperCollins Publishers, Inc., 1950.

Lewis, C.S. *The Chronicles of Narnia: The Silver Chair*. New York: HarperCollins Publishers, Inc., 1953.

Lewis, Gladys. "The Black Stallion and the Red Mare." *70 Favorite Stories for Young Readers*. New York: Reader's Digest Association, Inc., 1974.

Lincoln, Abraham. Quoted from Thinkexist.com. http://www.thinkexist.com (accessed April 12, 2010).

Lindgren, Astrid. *Pippi Longstocking*. New York: Penguin Books, 1950.

Lofting, Hugh. *The Story of Doctor Dolittle*. New York: William Morrow and Company, Inc., 1997.

London, Jack. *The Call of the Wild*. New York: Grosset and Dunlap, 1973.

Luther, Martin. Quoted from ThinkExist. http://www.thinkexist.com (accessed April 12, 2010).

MacLachlan, Patricia. *Sarah, Plain and Tall.* New York: Harper & Row Junior Books, 1985.

Montgomery, Lucy Maud. *Anne of Green Gables.* New York: Scholastic, Inc., 1989.

Morey, Walt. *Gentle Ben.* New York: E.P. Dutton, 1965.

O'Dell, Scott. *Island of the Blue Dolphins.* Boston: Houghton Mifflin Co., 1960.

O'Neill, Mary. *Hailstones and Halibut Bones: Adventures in Color.* New York: Bantam Doubleday Dell Publishing Group, Inc., 1989.

Paterson, Katherine. *Bridge to Terabithia.* New York: Harper & Row Publishing, Inc., 1977.

Paulsen, Gary. *Hatchet.* New York: Bradbury Press, 1987.

Paulsen, Gary. *Tracker.* New York: Bradbury Press, 1984.

Penn, William. Quoted from BrainyQuote. http://www.thinkexist.com (accessed April 12, 2010).

Peretti, Frank E. *The Secret of the Desert Stone.* Nashville: Thomas Nelson, Inc., 1996.

Petry, Ann. "Harriet Tubman: A Glory Over Everything." *Elements of Literature Introductory Course.* Austin: Holt, Rinehart and Winston, 1993.

Pfister, Marcus. *The Rainbow Fish.* New York: North-South Books, 1992.

Plato. *The Republic of Plato.* Edited by Elizabeth Watson Scharffenberger and Benjamin Jowett. Lyndhurst, NJ: Barnes and Noble, 2005.

Porter, Eleanor H. *Pollyanna.* New York: Penguin Putnam, 1994.

Potter, Beatrix. *The Tale of Benjamin Bunny.* New York: Viking Penguin, Inc., 1987.

Potter, Beatrix. *The Tale of Peter Rabbit.* New York: Viking Penguin, Inc., 1989.

Princeton Language Institute, *Roget's 21st Century Thesaurus in Dictionary Form.* Second Edition. Edited by Barbara Anne Kipfer. USA: Barnes & Noble, Inc., 1999.

Pudewa, Andrew. *Teaching Writing: Structure and Style Syllabus & Seminar Workbook.* Locust Grove, OK: Institute for Excellence in Writing, 2010.

Pyle, Howard. *The Merry Adventures of Robin Hood.* New York: Waldman Publishing Corp., 1985.

Rawls, Wilson. *Where the Red Fern Grows.* New York: Delacorte Press, 1996.

Rogers, Will. Quoted from BrainyQuote. http://www.brainyquote.com (accessed April 12, 2010).

Ruff, Howard. Quoted from ThinkExist. http://www.thinkexist.com (accessed April 28, 2010).

Ryrie, Charles Caldwell. *The Ryrie Study Bible: New American Standard.* Chicago: Moody Press, 1978.

Seuss, Dr. *How the Grinch Stole Christmas.* New York: Random House, Inc., 1957.

Seuss, Dr. *Horton Hears a Who.* New York: Random House, Inc., 1982.

Sewell, Anna. "The Adventures of Black Beauty." *The Bookshelf for Boys and Girls.* New York: The University Society, Inc., 1965.

Shakespeare, William. Quoted from BrainyQuote. http://www.brainyquote.com (accessed April 12, 2010).

Shaw, George Bernard. Quoted from Thinkexist.com. http://www.thinkexist.com (accessed April 12, 2010).

Shopenhauer, Arthur. Quoted from BrainyQuote. http://www.brainyquote.com (accessed April 12, 2010).

Sime, Richard, ed. *Elements of Literature Introductory Course.* Austin: Holt, Rinehart and Winston, 1993.

Smith, Carl B. *Helping Children Understand Literary Genres.* Bloomington, IN: ERIC Clearinghouse on Reading English and Communication, 1994.

Snicket, Lemony. *A Series of Unfortunate Events: Austere Academy.* New York: HarperCollins Publishers, Inc., 2000.

Snicket, Lemony. *A Series of Unfortunate Events: The Penultimate Peril.* New York: HarperCollins Publishers, Inc., 2005.

Stevenson, Robert Louis. *Kidnapped.* New York: Scholastic Inc., 2002.

Stoutenburg, Adrien. *Tall Tales.* Boston: Houghton Mifflin Company, 1989.

Sullivan, Anne. Quoted from BrainyQuote. http://www.brainyquote.com (accessed April 28, 2010).

Taylor, Helen L. *Little Pilgrim's Progress.* Chicago: Moody Press, 1987.

Taylor, Theodore. *The Trouble with Tuck.* New York: Doubleday & Company, Inc., 1981.

Ten Boom, Corrie. Quoted from ThinkExist.com. http://www.thinkexist.com (accessed April 12, 2010).

Thompson, Frank Charles. *Thompson Chain-Reference Bible: New International Version.* Michigan: B.B. Kirkbride Bible Co., 1983.

Tolkien, J. R. R. *The Hobbit.* New York: Ballantine Books, 1973.

Travers, P.L. *Mary Poppins.* San Diego: Harcourt Brace & Company, 1981.

Twain, Mark. "The Adventures of Tom Sawyer." *Elements of Literature Introductory Course.* Austin: Holt, Rinehart and Winston, 1993.

Untermeyer, Louis. "The Dog of Pompeii." *Elements of Literature Introductory Course.* Austin: Holt, Rinehart and Winston, 1993.

Washington, George. Quoted from BrainyQuote. http://www.brainyquote.com (accessed April 28, 2010).

Washington, Martha. Quoted from ThinkExist.com. http://www.thinkexist.com (accessed April 28, 2010).

White, E.B. *Charlotte's Web.* New York: HarperCollins Children's Books, 1952.

Whitman, Walt. "O Captain! My Captain!" *The Illustrated Treasury of Poetry for Children.* New York: Grossett and Dunlap, 1970.

Wordsworth, William. "Words About Kindness." CharacterCounts! http://charactercounts.org/ (accessed April 12, 2010).

Zeman, Anne and Kate Kelly. *Everything You Need to Know About English Homework.* New York: Scholastic, Inc., 1997.